the mother project

SOPHIE BERESINER

HarperCollins*Publishers*

HarperCollins*Publishers*
1 London Bridge Street
London SE1 9GF

www.harpercollins.co.uk

HarperCollins*Publishers*
1st Floor, Watermarque Building, Ringsend Road
Dublin 4, Ireland

First published by HarperCollins*Publishers* 2021

3 5 7 9 10 8 6 4 2

© Sophie Beresiner 2021

A catalogue record of this book is
available from the British Library

ISBN 978-0-00-845686-3

Printed and bound in Great Britain by
CPI Group (UK) Ltd, Croydon

MIX
Paper from
responsible sources
FSC C007454

This book is produced from independently certified FSC™ paper
to ensure responsible forest management.

For more information visit: www.harpercollins.co.uk/green

For Marlies.
You found me, in the end.
By whatever means you were always going to.

Contents

Prologue

This time last decade I was everything I needed to be. Only just thirty, new boyfriend after a four-year relationship hiatus ('Thank Christ,' said my concerned ovaries), becoming someone in an industry that is notoriously hard to break into and with wonderful hair that refused to cooperate in the best way possible. In fact I began 2010 celebrating my thirtieth birthday in a cottage with five of my friends. We were playing a last-decade board game called 'A Question Of Scruples' while we drank as much alcohol as our livers would allow. (Ha! We drank way more than that – we were only thirty once after all.) The game basically posed moral dilemmas on life, work, love et cetera, and players would guess each other's responses to win points. My new boyfriend picked a card from the deck and read aloud to his new audience: 'What would you do if you found out your girlfriend was infertile?'

I should add a caveat here that his nickname was 'Dad Jokes' and so, in an overexerted effort to be funny, he yelled, 'LEAVE HER!'

Um, LOL?

He wasn't hugely popular with my female friends that evening, and the men let him off with a yellow card, relieved that it wasn't them this time delivering the lead balloon that would put them in the doghouse. And today it's OK because we all still laugh about it. Because today I *am* infertile. Quite militantly so in fact. And he didn't leave me, he married me, probably to prove that he was joking after all, but maybe also because we fell madly in love.

It was funny to him at the time precisely because it seemed so unlikely. Needless to say, I didn't spend my childhood imagining infertility for myself. But, that's only the case until you end up on the wrong end of the fertility spectrum, do some research and discover that it actually affects one in seven couples and counting. Or talked to your friends about it and discovered that their routes to parenthood have, almost without exception, been nowhere near as easy as our old text books would have had us believe.

I certainly didn't expect to spend the entirety of my thirties battling cancer, regrowing my wonderfully unco-operative hair and then battling infertility – because make no mistake, it is a battle of epic proportions. Only to flop into a whole new decade ten years older, wiser, totally different and with the realisation that whatever happens next, I'll probably be aghast, appalled and amazed for the rest of all time.

When I decided to write a regular *Times* newspaper column about my surrogacy journey (I hate that word but there really is no other word that works as well as that one), it is because I was as interested in the journey (gah!) from the outside as I was dreading it from the inside. The hurdles we have faced emotionally are still smarting, but good God they're objectively interesting too. Writing in short recaps has led me to understand the breadth of the issues with women and our fertility. How perhaps reproducing is increasingly less compatible with our outrageously busy lives. And how in telling bits of my story, I've helped others understand or accept theirs.

With topics as divergent as infertility and surrogacy there will always be questions, and I think I have probably heard them all. So, here, for posterity (mine) and practicality (yours) I'd like to answer the big ones. The ones you've probably thought about yourself once or twice, or your friend or colleague, maybe your sister or aunt or maybe even me.

Dealing with infertility isn't easy, but it is definitely possible. With bells on in fact, because now that I'm here I couldn't imagine it any other way.

This is the story of my adventur– No, no, too rip-roaring. Of my experience? Nope, too emotionless. The story of my odysse– Way too ridiculously excessive. This is the story of my *journey*. I hope this telling – the in-depth one, the practical, pragmatic and personal one – will ultimately be a story of resilience and hope for anyone facing their own Mother Project.

1.

How do you know you're infertile?

Someone professionally straightforward tells you you're infertile, that's how you know. Perhaps in a medical facility of the standard nondescript variety, like this one I'm in right now. Nondescript, but already in the top two most hideous rooms I've ever sat in, nonetheless. Currently I can't hear anything except the whooshing of my own blood – that happens sometimes when you're delivered earth-tiltingly bad news that you weren't really expecting. Unfortunately, this ain't my first rodeo. My husband Mr B is definitely saying something soothing, because he's rubbing my back whilst doing so, but I'm deafened by hot white noise and instead focus on his adam's apple bobbing as he gulps something down repeatedly – ah yes, the taste of abject disappointment and distress. That's because this just happened:

'I'm afraid your ultrasound showed no ovarian function, in fact your left ovary was not visible at all. And your AMH and FSH blood test results also demonstrate that you are infertile.'

Infertile. A somewhat vague diagnosis that kind of makes the room warp in on itself while Mr B rubs my back, and no one rubs his. My hearing returns just in time to catch him saying, 'Well, you've been through worse, eh?' Oh Christ, I should have stayed deaf. In this moment, when I'm imagining my future hurtling down a toilet, it's safest to avoid comment. I glare at the poor man and then at the doctor. Dispassionate doctor with your face set to 'patiently waiting for news to register' whilst preparing leaflets on egg donation. OK, yes, I have – literally speaking – been through worse: the breast cancer, chemo and radiation that apparently fried my fertility and put me in this position in the first place. But still, I don't think it's appropriate to park me anywhere on the bad news emotional acceptance scale whilst I'm smack bang in the middle of processing this bit. Right now, as a woman finally ready to start celebrating my traitorous body again by making a baby with my lovely husband, *nothing* feels worse. I can't make a baby. My body has let me down again, and so I fucking hate my body right now, along with everyone else in this room. It's my right as a female human being. It's what *everyone* does. It's been my end goal, my dangling carrot to get me through the last five years of remission therapy, and now I'm here, I'm ready. And I can't do it?! OK, this may not literally be the worst thing in the world, but it's the worst thing in my world right now. This is just … well this is, just … this is not fucking FAIR.

2

Uh oh. I'm having an internal tantrum. I can feel the rage building at the same time I imagine the doctor going through his Kübler-Ross stages of grief checklist. 'She's skipped denial and gone straight to anger, so she'll be on to bargaining shortly, I'll wait.'

I'm not interested in bargaining. I want to go home and get into bed and cry for a hundred years. Instead I stand up abruptly and walk out of the room, while Mr B makes my apologies and follows me to the garden bench outside, where he disregards his own feelings to try and soothe mine. I know that this man crouching at my feet is the only person who understands what to do with me right now, he knows me better than anyone. He already understands that he said the wrong thing on the spur of the moment, and he's explaining that he panicked. He wanted nothing more than to shine some light onto a deeply dark situation, to put it into perspective in the only way he knew how. By telling me I'm not dying this time.

Yes. Yes that's true. *Sucks in deep breath*.

There is a similar kind of finality though. The no going backwards-ness. Once again my whole life has hit a trajectory I was not expecting, one I do not want, one that changes things forever. I'm angry at him because I won't ever see what my own child looks like, and he still might see his. And even as I'm thinking it, I know it's not fair. Even as I'm thinking it, I know it's *our* child I wanted to see, that beautiful and unique mix of me and him. And, if I can just clear some of this rage from behind my eyeballs, I can see that that's what he's lost too. Even right now, on this stupid garden bench, while I'm making a snotty spectacle of myself in front of the hospital-goers, and the doctor is still waiting for us inside.

Sucks in deeeep breath.

I close my eyes and stand up to give him the cuddle he also needs, and we go back in to talk over our options. Ha. I skipped depression and went straight to acceptance, Doc. I defied the linear laws of psychological grieving, now give me all the fucking egg donation leaflets so I can go home and cry for a hundred years.

In reality, I went back to work as if it were a routine blood test I'd just left the office for ('denial' you're thinking) and on the way I went about assessing what brought me here.

You would think that infertility after cancer is a given, but it really isn't. It depends on your cancer, your age, your treatment, your resilience, and I was reassured by my nurses that because I was only thirty at diagnosis, there was a strong chance of my reproductive system being spared, remaining unaffected. I guess because of my age I also had a strong chance of not being struck by cancer in the first place, so I shouldn't have rested so easily on those odds. In hindsight, I have to wonder if they were trying to appease themselves as much as me, because somewhere along the line, someone forgot to offer me my egg-freezing option. 'Sophie, you have cancer, we're going to ravage your body with toxins, would you like chocolate sprinkles and pre-emptive egg freezing with that?'

I'm not sure if I would even have said yes, knowing now that it would have delayed treatment by a few weeks. I was terrified and I wanted to put myself in the hands of the doctors, but to this day about 12 per cent of my midnight neuroses is dedicated to regretting that neglect. I wish I had had the information and the option. I might have been infertile, but I might also have had a portion of my own potential future preserved in a lab somewhere. At the very least, I would have had autonomy over making that decision and closing my own doors, rather than anger at whoever carelessly slammed them shut for me.

But that was then. Now, better, I genuinely thought I would be starting the IVF process after this appointment. A controlled conception because the logistics are a factor: I'm on ten years of endocrine therapy, meaning I have to take daily hormone pills to suppress the oestrogen that my cancer was receptive to. But if there is one key ingredient needed for baby making, it is oestrogen. My new hospital (I was rescued from the neglectful one by the Royal Marsden, but that's a whole other story) approved a one-year break in my treatment to try and start a family. I would do IVF to control the timescale. Around 80 per cent of couples fall pregnant naturally within a year of trying, but those stats don't work for someone with a hard deadline to get back on important medication, so assisted conception would save the day. I was to go and make sure everything was in order, and boom, we'd be on our way. When I took my last hormone tablet before the appointment, I remember thinking, 'Imagine! I'll have a two-month-old baby by the time I have to take another one of these.' Ha!

I have a fistful of leaflets in my bag, so I start to skim them. I have the option to try carrying my own child, an embryo created by introducing my husband's sperm to an egg donated by a stranger. In which case, maybe I still *could* have a two-month-old baby in a year. How long does this egg donation process take? I recognise that my Kübler-Ross acceptance model may not fit the linear path of least resistance, but my psyche still ticks those bloody boxes. This is the bargaining part. I recognise it because I do it all the time; I bargain with myself in order to move on from the scariest part as fast as possible. It's a well-practised subconscious method. If I slow it down and write it out, it works something like this:

BAD NEWS! The worst news, in fact. How will I ever feel OK again?

Me, to myself: 'You need a plan. A quick and foolproof plan that means this needn't be the worst news after all and you can be yourself again as quickly as possible. Shove it in a box, as they say.'

Me, back to myself: 'OK plan plan plan, ah! So I can't have my own genetically related child with my husband, but – and at this point this feels kind of gross – I could still have *another person's* child with him. How about that?'

Me again: 'You're right, there is something gross about that. But crucially, don't tell anyone it feels gross because they'll judge you. How about we reframe it as "I could still have *a* child with my husband?"'

Me: 'How about I could still have *my* child, and skip straight to the accepted part of acceptance? Be done with all this unnecessary gut-wrenching? You'll feel that way in the end anyway.'

Me: 'Deal!'

Smashed it.

And so, with a bargaining (that in retrospect looks suspiciously like denial) plan in place, I *am* able to go back to work after the appointment. I am able to be totally normal and effective in meetings. It's just a pure coincidence that when a colleague booked fish for the photo shoot catering, knowing full well that I don't eat fish, that I lost it. And, um, when she argued with me in a meeting room, it was a totally unconnected resulting panic attack that made me shut myself in there so no one else could make me feel bad today. Must be my time of the month, eh? Oh wait, I don't have those anymore. I'm infertile, remember?

In some situations, a plan is not enough to paper the cracks. You can't kid the kid-less, this situation is quite horrible. Not horrible like I'd imagined when I sometimes thought of other people being infertile, like Charlotte from *Sex and the City*, say. But worse. It's worse than that, because it's me. I am the centre of my own universe and my universe just got sucked into a black hole. There is nothing for it but to go home and mourn what we both just lost, together.

When I finally crawl into bed and cry into my husband's neck, I feel better because I'm there, but I can't seem to stop. It's the plan. It's sort of stuck in the back of my throat. I'm crying about my past and my future at the same time. We're going to need more tissues.

At some point during my treatment – it's hazy, because that is what chemo does to your memory – I found myself in the mahogany-panelled office of a fertility doctor, prompted by my kind breast-care nurse and my sister. The former suggested I might want to speak to someone about starting a family once all of this grim, life-saving treatment was over. The latter, because my sister, Amy, had offered to freeze her own eggs in lieu of anyone offering to freeze mine. Amy is four years older than me, she has two beautiful daughters, and I knew that in the case of my own eggs being off the menu, as it were, hers would be the next best thing. It felt hopeful and lovely.

So, I was quite thrown when this particular expert told me he very rarely worked on cases of intra-familial egg donation. 'What?' I said. 'Surely that's the most obvious and common solution. Surely that's the closest infertile people get to ever having their own genetic children?'

And therein lies the obvious issue. 'Think about Christmas,' he told me. 'Your whole family gathered in one place. Think about the times your child – because this *will* happen – tells you he hates you and runs to his auntie for a cuddle. Think about a scenario where you want to discipline your child and your sister chastises you for it, or makes any comment on your parenting whatsoever. It's common among normal families, of course, but in this case that kind of behaviour would have such extreme connotations.'

Click! Of course.

I went home and repeated the obvious flaw in our thinking to my husband. 'Thank god,' he said. 'I did not want to have a baby with your sister.' It was funny at the time, but even that comment sucked me into a thought tornado for a few days. He had gone along with my emotionally charged plan B because he knew I needed it, even though he had an uncomfortable gut-reaction. But how do you say that to someone you love in that kind of situation? It's intricate and messy and primed for an explosion. I appreciated his stance as soon as the doctor cleared the sentimental detritus and let me see it logically, but what if he hadn't? Would Mr B have said no further down the line? Or would he have gone along with it and compromised his own instinct. Either option is insurmountable, so we would have been somewhat screwed.

The doctor had explained to me that it is possible, of course, but we would all three have to have separate counselling, group counselling, and something about presenting our case to some kind of ethics committee to consider the moral and psychological implications. I've researched it since and I can't find any set precedent on whether or not he was entirely right. Except for one study that mentioned some UK clinics operating a pool egg donation system, offering recipients a choice of using their relative's egg (generally a sister's) or that of an unknown donor from the pool. Interestingly, most people chose the stranger.

There are many pro schools of thought when it comes to sibling egg donation, and many against, but in the end it's kind of moot. My husband and I always seem to agree on the big stuff, and we'd independently realised this was not the way for us to go. Thank you Amy, it was an amazing gesture and we're forever grateful, but you don't need to procreate with my husband. Chances are, I'd be able to do it myself when the time comes anyway, I'd thought.

But the time came, and I can't, so here we are. Crying in bed, considering our options. Now the tables have turned a little. I know egg donation is our next best option, but currently my gut reaction is similar to his when he was going to have a baby with my sister. My instinct is to not say it out loud. Bury it. Bury it. Bury it Sophie. It's not a nice stance to have, it's an amazing, fantastical, progressive opportunity and I feel … jealous. Which makes me feel ugly. And so I cry a bit more and say it out loud, 'I'm sorry, I just don't want to have to have someone else's baby in my belly. It feels gross. I don't know why I feel like this.'

Mr B looks at me and says the very thing that lets me know I was right to marry him. 'I know. It's because it is a bit gross.' Oh my God, he gets it. It's a similar thing, he is adjusting to this infertility diagnosis. It's a massive discombobulating lurch for him too. He loves me, he loves my face (thank you for that), he wants to have a baby with me, he wants it to have my eyes or my smile and definitely not his nose, but he wants it to be ours. There is a lot of emotional adjustment to considering an alternative route to baby making. The semantics are tricky to get your head around. There is guilt in suggesting a child made up of anything other than our combination of genes would not be 'our child', but it takes some getting used to. Of course, people adopt children and they are a million per cent their children, but it doesn't happen overnight. It took those altruistic people a little while to get there, too.

So to Mr B, mixing his sperm with some strange woman's egg also feels a bit gross. It's like the result of some clinically supervised cheating.

Right now, at around eleven in the evening on D-for-diagnosis-day, there is no reasoning or rational thinking or room for debate. There is just infertility and exhausted, reluctant acknowledgment. And so we fall asleep

By five the next morning, when I wake up in that delicious second of peace and calm before reality whooshes in, I have an indeterminate tingle in my belly. Just a tiny one. But is it revulsion or rapture? Revulsion, definitely. But also something else. Something like ... wonder maybe? And then it is gone again.

When I was first sick and very, very scared, Mr B and I would sleep holding hands. Night-time was the most distressing time for me, it's when the worst fear settled in and I'd always dread waking up with that same awful realisation every day. So Mr B would hold my hand until I fell asleep and we'd stay that way until I woke up.

I instinctively reach for his hand now, and I realise that this is really quite bad actually. This is not my rightful prize. I should be awarded something pretty epic after beating cancer, successfully growing all my hair back and re-establishing someone resembling my old self in this new life. Not infertility for fuck's sake. Not familiar middle-of-the-night fear for my future. I should've forgotten what that feels like by now, surely, rather than be right back in that place again.

Mr B doesn't stir, but he squeezes my hand back, out of some sad muscle memory, and eventually I fall asleep again, like that, until we wake up the same position.

It is a more godly hour of the morning when I wake up properly (ahh, a new day! WHOOSH, oh yeah. Infertile), and there's that tingle back again. Definitely more erring away from revulsion this time. Definitely leaning more towards marvel at the wonder of modern medicine. That there can be such amazing options for people like me. Imagine! Imagine if someone cut off your arm and then said, 'Here, take mine, I don't need it,' and then you went through a protracted process to clip it into place and voilà, a working arm, but with someone else's fingernails and hairs. Different. Not the arm you were born with, but you wouldn't say no, right? Really, it's quite incredible. The fact that my poor, lonely womb could welcome this unusual result of a passionate petri-dish rendezvous. Wow. It's like not actually being infertile at all, right? If I can be pregnant, have a viable pregnancy, feel kicking and morning sickness and let my DNA merge with my baby – oops! I said MY baby. It's happening without me even trying, I'm coming to terms with the idea! The petri-dish rendezvous part I could definitely do without. It is possible – in case you were wondering – to have pre-emptive relationship jealousy about your husband's sperm. But then I am a Scorpio, so maybe being a bit extra in that department is to be expected. Would having another woman's gamete mixing with my husband's sperm be all that bad? Would it? Yes. Yes it would because it's not fair that it can't be mine. So OK, I'm not quite there yet. I need another bout of crying and to mainline some Malbec, and then we'll see.

It's only the next morning, when I'm gazing lovingly at my cat Woody, that something shifts. Woody insists on nestling into my armpit when I sleep. He's not allowed in the bedroom, but he howls his way in because he needs to be next to me. It's the sweetest thing, and I can't resist, and so I get a bad night's sleep while he intermittently stomps across my chest to get to the other armpit, and Mr B remains blissfully oblivious. It's because Woody chooses me. He loves Mr B, but for some reason he needs me more. And just to be clear here, Woody is a cat. An entirely different species, who I would run into a burning building to protect. He doesn't have my genes, he doesn't have my eyes or my character traits. Or my language skills or the requisite number of legs to qualify him for this next statement, but I love him more than is humanly possible. He isn't even made up of half of my husband and I feel that way, so how the hell could there be any revulsion about the idea of carrying and nurturing a human person who is? Ding! Oh my God! I excitedly shake Mr B awake and tell him I am IN LOVE with the idea of egg donation. And I genuinely mean it. The wonder! The marvel! The RAPTURE. I can suddenly and clearly imagine leaning into a cot in the room next door and scooping up a little person who looks something like him. I can actually joyfully picture my future, and so therefore I must be psychic and this must be the way it will be.

Infertility needn't be the full stop we all presume it to be. It doesn't have to spell prolonged heartbreak and ruin lives, and it sure as hell is not a patch on cancer in the misery stakes. Not three days after this diagnosis in my case, anyway. We can and will do this and it is going to be wonderful because there is no space in my battered heart for anything else. Kübler-Ross, I win. I'm at the acceptance stage and I didn't even dawdle in depression.

Really, it's quite simple. Cancer stole my fertility, and so I am on a mission to steal it back. Sort of.

I will use someone else's eggs, and I will be excited about it. I am excited about this, medicine is fucking amazing. Let's go.

2.

How does egg donation work?

Having never considered the possibility of using someone else's eggs to make my own baby until I was point blank confronted with it, there is an entire moral and emotional conundrum to navigate before we even get into the logistics. And the logistics here in the UK are janky, to say the least. In my desperately naive mind, there is a raft of egg donor banks where virile young women queue up to deposit their unwanted egg reserves in exchange for some money towards their student loan. And then I realise I am thinking of the cliched notion of the student sperm donor, rather than using any actual biological reasoning, and so I shake my head and start again. For one, women produce one solitary egg per month, rather than the one billion sperm men shed in the same time span. Women have a finite supply of eggs over their reproductive lifetime, and the process of extracting them is – in the pleasure stakes – about as far away from wanking into a cup as it's possible to be. So already, I understand that of course there is a serious dearth of egg donors in the UK. Furthermore, the whole process takes a good few weeks, there are definite health risks, you undergo general anaesthesia for the actual egg collection procedure, and you cannot be compensated any more than £750 for the pleasure. Does it seem worth it? Oh, don't get me wrong, it absolutely is worth it. If you could see my face right now, the renewed hope of a dejected infertile woman, with the new knowledge that there are some exceptionally wonderful women who are willing to offer their eggs to help me?

So it was with this renewed hope that Mr B and I found ourselves in the plush Harley Street offices of Dr Flannery, consultant gynaecologist and expert in reproductive medicine. He's the guy that diagnosed me as infertile in that horrible hospital room in the first place, but now we're in his private office (the free-IVF postcode lottery does not accept members of the Cancer Survival Society). I've forgiven him for ripping my heart out of my uterus, and I'm feeling increasingly warmer towards him as we go over our options. For about a minute and a half, until he explains to me that donor anonymity was abolished in the UK in 2005, so the current waiting list for a suitable match is up to two years long. Which, with my medically imposed deadline to get back on my remission drugs in place, is about two years too long. It's not his fault, but if the same person keeps delivering bad news to me on repeat, it's hard for me to regard them fondly. WHAT DOES THIS EVEN MEAN? I ask much more calmly than my internal caps lock suggests. 'Basically, any donor-conceived person has the right to find out identifying information about the person who donated the gamete once they turn eighteen. It means you could donate eggs, then have someone knock on your door a couple of decades later asking to know all about you, their biological parent.'

Needless to say, the already small pool of donors quickly dried up after the anonymity act came into play, and things became extra difficult for people like me. It is an ethically motivated step change to allow a child to know their genetic make-up in case of illness, or basic and understandable curiosity, say, and it really makes sense in lots of ways. Not least, it eradicates the risk of having a sexual relationship with the guy you just fell in love with, who actually turns out to be your brother because neither of you had any idea you were both conceived by anonymous egg donation, from the same donor, and you happen to have lived round the corner from each other all these years. Phew!

If time is not on your side, like me, there are specialist agencies that help by recruiting and matching you with egg donors, with only a three- to six-month wait, but you need to pay a sizeable agency fee up front, on top of the IVF costs to cover the egg stimulation and extraction treatment. And suddenly it all starts to feel insurmountable again. No! Oh no, no. I can't deal with a full stop already.

Dr Flannery explains that IVF abroad is increasing in popularity, with our laws, prices, processes and small donor egg pool driving people out of our country. When you put it like that, it doesn't feel ideal, but right now it feels necessary, and I *do* love to travel. He explains that there are three options for us: Russia, America and Spain. There are other countries that support egg donation IVF of course, but the way Harley Street works is on a partnerships basis. Since the treatment would be international – in that part of it would be done here (the 'monitoring' part) and part in whatever clinic in whatever country we go for (the 'paramount' part) – doctors here work together with preferred partner clinics, and Dr Flannery has one in each of those countries. There are various reasons to go to various places, but it is widely known that America represents the 'gold standard' because assisted conception is big business over there. It costs a lot and you get what you pay for, timeframe, professionalism and experience-wise. Spain is definitely less expensive than the States. They have strict regulations whereby the clinics alone know the identity of the donors that they match you with. In Russia it is decidedly less expensive and yeah, OK, less regulated, but how bad can it be, eh?

Dr Flannery recommends that we go to America. 'OK, America, great! Oh sweet relief, a plan. So, how much on average would it cost to do egg donation IVF in the States?' He tells us, without blinking, that it's somewhere in the region of fifty to sixty thousand pounds. My jaw makes its way to the floor and Dr Flannery sits and waits for me to collect myself. He doesn't seem to have too many concerns that money might be an issue for some of his clients. Re-looking around the mahogany office, I can understand why, and I sort of feel embarrassed. Like when you pick up an outfit in a fancy store and try not to visibly balk at the price tag. I'm also thinking the American clinic he refers his patients to probably pays for the Chelsea Harbour yacht moorings I imagine he has, and that there is no way on earth we can find that kind of money, so how about Spain or Russia?

It feels so ridiculously unfair that we're even talking about having to spend a very healthy annual salary on my failed ovaries because I HAD CANCER. I'm not being frivolous here, I don't want to buy a Couture Chanel gown (well, of course I do, but not in the context of this conversation) or a 160th of a yacht (I looked it up, yachts are on average 160 times more expensive than donor egg treatment in the States). I want to be a mother. That's all. Please. Why can my colleague get her IVF treatment free because she had unexplained infertility, but I have to remortgage my house to do it because I can explain mine. It was cancer, guys. Can I catch a break now please?

Spain, it turns out, is also quite expensive because frankly any scenario you can imagine discussing in this office will need an extra zero on the end. I'm literally negotiating countries at this point, so Russia, bottom of Dr Flannery's list, actually seems to make the most sense for us, not least financially. The parts that are instantly appealing are, in no particular order, the fact that they have retained donor anonymity laws, so the donor pool should be bigger and more immediately available. Can I take this opportunity to remind us all of my Royal Marsden enforced baby-making deadline – it's short. And stressful. So yes, Russia, you were saying? There is also the option of 'non-anonymous' gamete donation, so in theory we would have more options about the path we want to take because the issue of anonymity will undoubtedly come up with our own kid one day when it wants to know who, if not me, created it. I will just stick a pin in that thought for now, thanks. So, Russia, you were saying? They offer more affordable medical and fertility programmes than the West according to Dr Flannery, and they also offer a population that bears more resemblance to me than I realised until we started trying to 'match features' on the example donor database later that day. But we'll get to that.

My heritage is Russian, you see. My paternal grandfather, Lazar, was born in Simferopol, capital of the Republic of Crimea, and yes, Beresiner is a Russian name. It's actually – funny story – the name of the river in Belarus where Napoleon was overcome. So since then *Bérézina* has been used in colloquial French as a synonym for 'catastrophe'. Yep, at this point that seems about right.

When I explained my thinking to Dr Flannery, he introduced us to his Russian clinic counterpart, Dr Sokolov, and we set about getting the ball rolling. Finally! Action! And progress. We actually left that appointment with a hopeful spring in our step and made a new appointment, with a bottle of wine and a laptop on our kitchen table to search through the Russian clinic's egg donor database. And this is precisely where egg donation gets quite surreal.

The clinic coordinator sent us a link to search through the database of donors who basically match my feature requirements. That is, pale, dark hair, dark eyes, slim build, tallish. The database is anonymous; there are no names or distinguishing information, but there are baby pictures and, woah, some of them – traditional Russian outfits aside – could have been mine. This is actually the first time I've ever considered that my features were anything other than familial. Nope. Turns out, they're decidedly Russian. Which feels hugely reassuring and calming right now. This, on top of the 7,500 euros egg donation package they offer, feels like an infertility win. OK, it could be the wine, but when we send our downpayment to the clinic that evening, I am positively giddy.

It feels like such a short amount of time later that we are planning our first trip to St Petersburg. The clinic coordinator was busy putting our egg donor match into process. Once they've successfully matched us, they can go about starting the egg stimulating cycle – exactly the same as any IVF treatment here in the UK, just minus the part where they put the embryo back in. That's where I come in. We will never know anything more about our donor other than her medical history, education and profession, a little note about why she wants to donate her eggs and her baby picture. I feel huge surges of gratitude for this international incognito saviour, this is starting to feel possible now. We've already come so far from that day in the hospital when I thought I had no hope of becoming a mother.

And then, before I know it, after a flurry of interminably long visa applications and flight bookings, we're touching down in St Petersburg and making our way directly from the airport to the clinic for our initial consultation.

My Russian is minimal. OK, it's microscopic. OK, I know Спасибо means 'thank you', but I have no idea how to pronounce, it so I remain mute and use the universal language of pointing at the Google Translate app instead. And Uber (thank God for Uber). And so here we are! Outside a crumbly pharmacy that seems to share the same address as the clinic. It's, um, pretty dingy inside, and when I point to the address on my phone and am shooed towards an unmarked brown door in the back, I start to feel uncomfortable.

But still – this is it! Must conjure hope! And excitement! Mr B and I are met by an imposing looking member of staff with a face mask on, and silently guided to a tiny waiting area in the corridor and, oh man, do I feel uneasy. It's just that it all seems very 'back door' (um, we *literally* accessed it through a back door). I'm really not feeling sure about this and just as I open my mouth to worry at Mr B, I'm whisked away from him by another clinic staffer, who apparently speaks as much English as my Russian. I don't have the opportunity or the lingual ability to voice any concerns as I'm ushered into a tiny room and asked – I think – to undress.

I am standing, holding my proffered pile of surgical attire, in the corner of a cubicle that manages to feel clinical and chintzy at the same time. There are two beds with frilly floral sheets, one of which, to my absolute horror, is already occupied by a nervous-looking Russian patient in paper knickers. Apparently I have no choice but to self-consciously strip and put on my own paper gown and pants, and apprehensively sit and wait on the bed. This is like being checked into infertility prison.

We sit about a foot apart and resolutely avoid eye contact until I'm collected and deposited in the next room for the most tortuous internal examination of my life. Not one recognisable word has yet been exchanged, yet here I am, in a strange clinic in a strange country with my legs in stirrups and a stranger peering between them. It's no wonder my body forcibly ejects the speculum she isn't holding onto while she reaches for something else. It hits her hard in the chest and clatters to the floor. Mortified, I try to apologise, but I don't have my translate app to point to, so instead I resolutely avoid eye contact until she's done. I cannot wait to run away from this place, fast.

But then Mr B and I are reunited outside, and finally we meet our consultant, Dr Sokolov. It's amazing what speaking the same language does to appease a situation. The relief actually makes me feel ignorant, like I'm gate-crashing this foreign country and I'm expecting everyone to make *me* feel at home. But to be honest, there is a precarious vulnerability around our reason for being here, and just having someone understand what I'm saying is like a soothing tincture. I'll take it.

Dr Sokolov is imposing but we reframe it as impressive. She is brusque, to the point, very obviously intelligent and medically accomplished, and so we invest blind trust and hope in her helping us. Because she tells us she will give us a baby.

As we fill the taxi back to our hotel with nervous chatter, we convince each other that her manner was just lost in translation. We're doing this! We have a plan in place and a schedule to prepare for and I'm going to carry a flipping baby with a history so diverse and exciting I can't wait to tell him or her all about it. I have about nine months left on my year-long cancer medication break. The timing is just about perfect. Ah, yes. Everything is going exactly to plan …

But (oh, there's always a 'but') hang on, what's that? A spanner in the works as soon as we've set the wheels in motion? About a month later, well into my treatment plan by now, I need a minor operation that might potentially impact my timeline.

Oh sigh. On my birthday the year after I finished chemo for breast cancer, I got a letter from the NHS telling me that, as I knew from my smear test results, I would need an operation to remove the high-grade level 3 abnormal cells holding my cervix hostage. Only I didn't know. My doctor hadn't managed to feed that back before I got the letter. It's not the kind of news a cancer survivor relishes on her birthday. But it was fine, really. The operation was successful, if terrifying, and I've been all clear ever since. Only now it seems it's left some scarring that, years later, would make an embryo transfer procedure impossible. So I'll need it removed. Oh sigh.

It's nothing big, but any international IVF schedule needs to be synchronised and consistent, so we really need to find out if it's going to be a problem. Apparently there is a peculiar time of the year when everyone involved in the Sophie Beresiner Treatment Plan, from both sides of the hemisphere, happen to go on holiday at the same time, and it is right now.

I *really* need some advice and information because we've already got our visa and booked our flights for the embryo transfer in Russia, so should I try to cancel? Will my dates change and, if so, should my hormone medication protocol change?

But I get an anxiety-inducing out-of-office automated email from Dr Sokolov. And then one from the clinic's international client coordinator when I try her next. This is absolute panic stations. I totally understand that people need their holidays, but couldn't any of them have warned me in advance? I send all my urgent questions again to Dr Sokolov, pleading for a response, and after a good day and a half of refreshing my inbox, she gives me one:

> Hello Sophie. I've forwarded your email to Dr Flannery.

Dr Flannery responds immediately. Sort of.

> Dr Flannery is on annual leave and will not return until the end of the month. For all urgent enquiries, please contact your international client coordinator.

And just as I'm about to tumble into a heap of neglected foreboding, my husband swoops in to take charge. He is exceptionally good at that. He's the assertive orderliness to my emotional chaos.

And so he sends an assertive and orderly email to Dr Sokolov to reaffirm our precarious position and appeal to her better nature. It went like this:

> Hi Dr Sokolov. With all due respect I hope we are not expected to wait for a gentleman to return from his vacation in order to get answers to our urgent questions. Is there anyone else who can help us?

Uh oh, it seems we poked the bear. Until now I didn't realise doctors were allowed to get pissy with their patients.

> This 'gentleman on vacation' has arranged an operation
> for you while still being on vacation. I am sending mails to
> you while still being on vacation, with my two children.

(Ooph, burn.)

> I will discuss your case with our medical ethics committee
> after my vacation and will discuss with you after I have
> spoken to them.

Hmm. I'm not quite sure why an ethics committee needs to discuss my treatment protocol, but we find out two weeks later when she Skypes us. From the off I feel like I'm convincing my boss to let me keep my job. I start by beaming at her that my UK doctors all said the operation was fine, it hasn't affected anything, and we're all good to go ahead with the original embryo transfer date! Isn't that great?!

She remains deadpan while she delivers the news that after speaking with the ethics committee, the clinic was no longer willing to work with us. There would be no embryo transfer. I can't remember the last time I felt this floored. Utterly gobsmacked, overwrought about how much of our strict timeline has already been spent at this clinic, about our perfect donor match, about the huge deposit we've paid. I implore her to give me a reason. 'I am not willing to discuss this with you any further,' she says again and again, until we literally get on our knees and beg, and then she gives the real reason. 'I did not like

27

the tone of your emails.' What? WHAT? Sobbing, I tell her that she is playing God. 'You see?' she says. 'You can't handle it. And you will just blame me when you don't manage to get pregnant, because you won't.'

Well, that was a Skype session that will necessitate some years of therapy. I've since discovered that Dr Sokolov did something similar to another British patient, stopping her treatment when it looked like her case would be slightly more difficult because of a minor medical issue, but accusing her of being a drug addict instead. With the exception of the ones prescribed for her IVF, this patient had never touched drugs in her life. I suspect Dr Sokolov is on a mission to protect her success statistics, wiping out anyone who threatens to knock a few points off. It baffles me how anyone who chooses to work in the business of baby making can be that heartless. Fertility doctor does not equal a good person. And I spent a long time trying to understand that, because surely her unregulated treatment of us goes against some sort of moral code. HAH ha ha, my God. I was so naive. I've since met *so* many more.

Which brings me back to Dr Flannery. I sent a frantic email explaining what I'm sure he already knew: that we had been unceremoniously dumped for a personal reason, not a medical one. He scheduled us in for another office consultation in two agonisingly long weeks' time. We got the bill before we got the appointment.

*   *   *

I would be five months into my one-year baby-making window before we managed to start again, so you see, already the maths wasn't going to work out. I moved on from Dr Flannery as soon as I became paranoid that it was in his financial interest for our case to keep not working out. When we finally made it to his office, and recounted the whole sorry story, his reaction was unsympathetic. He brushed it under the very expensive Persian carpet, suggested we move on and find somewhere else, and again recommended the American colleagues that we could afford even less now, after the chunk of money this useless advice session just cost us. Dr Flannery was careless in every sense of the word.

I may have wasted a chunk of time and money, but moving on and finding our new consultant, Mr Hiyer, was a revelation. I loved him from the moment he sweetly proffered a tissue after I sobbed through my backstory thus far. 'Well,' he said, smiling reassuringly, 'I think we can do better than that.'

I let out the breath I'd been holding since this whole debacle began.

3.
What is IVF abroad really like?

This time I found the clinic. Mr Hiyer had his partner practices too and he gently suggested America was a good option in terms of their regulations and success rates, especially taking into account the experience we'd just had, but he absolutely understood our position too. We are sticking with Russia because we have mentally and financially established our procreating plan there. The donor part of donor egg IVF becomes so important emotionally. I wasn't expecting it, but it's the bit that replaces me, essentially. So yes the States might be 'better' and, yes, Spain might be clearer cut, but I've seen pictures and thought about my heritage, and a Russian donor, the 'me' part, it just feels right. But we did our due diligence this time. We researched, we read reviews, we Skyped the new clinic and subjected them to a Mr B interrogation, and then we felt comfortable that this was the one. In actual fact, fuck that, we felt outraged that this wasn't the one in the first place. Why were we sent to Dr Sokolev when this was an option? Mr Hiyer was happy to work with a clinic beyond his partnership repertoire, totally supportive in fact, keen even to meet his counterpart at this new Creation Clinic and get the ball rolling. Thank whatever higher powers for Mr Hiyer. Again, we book our flights, apply for our visas and make our way to Russia.

On that. Getting a visa to travel to Russia is like completing a challenge in *The Crystal Maze*. First, you have to not succumb to website sharks who manage to hit the top spot in Google Search and con you by over-charging for an unofficial service that looks like the official one, but isn't. Argh, game over. Player One, play again? Yes please, it's urgent.

Then you have to fill out – accurately and truthfully because we're under the impression this will all be checked and verified by the visa adjudicators – the last ten years of travel. Exact dates and destinations, please. GAH! I travel a lot, for work, for pleasure, OK this might take some time. And some forensic analysis of the blurry stamps in my last two passports. Then the medical and financial history of your entire family (alright, not exactly, but almost) and, finally, 73 pages later, you're good. Oh wait! You have to make your excuses at work and go to the embassy to put your paperwork through. But why is the door not opening? WHY IS THE DOOR NOT OPENING? You see a sign informing you that today is one of sixteen Russian National Holidays – of course it is Player One, why didn't you do your Russian Public Holiday research before you rescheduled your meetings and travelled across London to get your visa? Better luck next time. Player Two? You're up.

Player Two, Mr B, makes it into the building the next day, he takes his paper number ticket and waits one hour, forty minutes until he is called. He has used the wrong date format for his years of education and so he has to pay £12 to use the waiting room computer, pay £6 to print the new paperwork, take another ticket and wait another hour for his turn and … and … 'Your photo does not cover the requisite 50 per cent of the photo area.' Please find a photo booth, come back, take a ticket, wait your turn.

Player One, Round Two!

This would be our second trip to Russia, you'd think we'd be well versed in visa acquisition by now, but nope. There is apparently a limit to how many tourist visas you're allowed in one year, but it should be fine, right? We shouldn't need too many trips and, besides, I have to be back on my endocrine medication within that time, too. My hospital was comfortable about extending my 'break' by six months, which takes me up to the end of the year. So here we go again. Visas finally approved, tickets booked, take off, turbulence, tears, touch down!

Creation Clinic is only a couple of miles from Dr Sokolov's, but it feels like another world entirely. Everything is bright and white, the staff are immaculate, they're helpful (they even picked us up from the airport!), they all speak English and they use it to demonstrate how encouraging and lovely they all are. My consultant, Dr Irina, is calm and kind and I cannot quite believe this is the experience that was available to me from the beginning. Why did I draw such a short straw first time around?

We already have a new donor, this time from a frozen egg bank, so the eggs are there, ready to get busy with Mr B's own, ahem, deposit. We crossed the t's and dotted the i's and made the all-important, deposit (I say 'we' ...), and then we were free to have a lovely wander round St Petersburg in the snow. Man, that place is beautiful, especially at night. All the streetlamps shine with this wonderful warm light, and the architecture is breathtaking. There are these little arched bridges over the canals everywhere, it's just so romantic. If the precarious icicles overhead didn't pose an immediate death threat, this would be like walking in a Disney movie. It all helps towards investments in the Hope Bank this time around.

The trip was definitely magical, and then it was over. After a jubilant plane ride home, we were back and once again, full of ticklish excitement. It's almost addictive, this rollercoaster of emotions. The lows make you really appreciate and pin hopes on the highs so much more. It's the rocket fuel that spurs us on, and there is so much to hope for right now that I don't know quite what to do with myself. What to pray for first on the agenda is the embryo count. Following that laboratory liaison, we are waiting for a phone call, sometime in the next five days, that will tell us how many of the donor eggs were fertilised. How many survived the all-important five days that then qualifies them as Strong Blastocysts. Basically, how many chances we have to succeed. Pass me the wine, for goodness' sake.

At this point, after discussing our best route to success with both Mr Hiyer and Dr Sokolov, we've decided to do Preimplantation Genetic Diagnosis, or PGD, on our embryos. Ah yes, we've chosen to intervene scientifically a bit more here. There are 'upgrade options' for IVF patients that make particular sense when you have a short time frame, say, or have had repeated miscarriages. I'm not a scientist so I won't go into it too deeply, but by whatever means of creating perfectly healthy-seeming embryos you choose – naturally or assisted – about a third will have some chromosomal abnormality that the body will try to eliminate by way of rejection (aka failed pregnancy or miscarriage). It explains the high rate of miscarriage that exists in that first 12 weeks before you can let the world know that you're pregnant.

So it makes sense to offer the option of PGD to anyone undergoing IVF who is concerned about passing on a genetic disease or disorder. Or to anyone who is investing a significant amount of money, has a very specific and tight deadline and, therefore, wants to maximise their chances of success. Moi. It means that we know we will only be transferring chromosomally 'perfect' embryos, so we are armed with useful information before we even start. Namely, if my body rejects them, it won't be because there was something 'wrong' with the embryo. At Creation Clinic it costs around a grand per embryo, but we've already invested so much just to get here so, really, if it will up our chances, then it seems to make sense.

So this is where we're at: after the petri-dish dance among twelve donor eggs from donor no. 1002 and Mr B's sperm, we had eleven embryos. Eleven! (I wonder how many embryos *my* eggs would have made. Obviously way more because Mr B and I already have chemistry on our side.)

After five days of waiting for them to turn into day-five blastocysts, only the strongest, winning embryos survive. We have nine blastocysts. Woohoo! Now is when they do the PGD testing. Now is when we sit at home in England, drinking wine and watching the phone. And a little later is when we receive the call to tell us that six of the little guys made it to status: Perfection. That means six goes at doing this thing. It also means six of my future babies are sitting in a freezer in St Petersburg, waiting for me to welcome them into my womb. Ooh, I have to sit down. This is overwhelmingly lovely. I am full, FULL of love for those little bundles of cells. It's not anything I was expecting to feel at this point, and it might be the wine, but it hits me full in the face; I've come so far. These aren't even viable yet and I actually genuinely love them. Are they lonely? I wonder. In the Russian freezer? OK yes, it's the wine. I'm putting it down now. Goodnight.

*　*　*

Dr Irina and Mr Hiyer spend the next month synchronising my cycle, and then Mr B and I get back on a plane for the third and final time (wish wish, pray pray) for the Frozen Embryo Transfer, or FET in IVF forum language. Essentially, the embryo transfer is the same whichever country you do it in. On a very specific day of your IVF treatment cycle you go to the clinic, where your embryo has been successfully defrosted within the last two hours. You drink till your bladder is uncomfortably full because it makes for a clearer ultrasound image, you get into surgical scrubs, leave your husband at the door (I think this is exclusive to Russia) and you imagine that this very moment – this one right here – will be the moment that changes everything, forever.

How awesome is that? The actual process is relatively painless, like a longer, drawn-out smear test but with more people in the room and a stronger urge to pee. It's amazing, anxiety-inducing, stupendously emotional and incredibly weird all at once. Dr Irina talks me through everything that's happening as she finds just the right spot in my uterus to deposit my embryo. I feel the weight of all the prep on my shoulders.

Did I do my injections right? How did anyone give me – a total needle-phobe – that responsibility? What if I messed it up and now my chemically enhanced endometrium isn't inviting enough? I think my face speaks volumes as one of the nurses squeezes my hand, brushes my cheek and kindly murmurs something totally unintelligible in my ear. I wish I understood Russian. Dr Irina barks another unknown instruction at the wall, a little hatch opens and a human arm passes through holding my embryo in a catheter. You see? Awesome! Traditional baby making might feel somewhat nicer, physically, but it definitely is not as fascinating as this.

I actually feel lucky right now. Dr Irina shows me on the screen as the little embryo whooshes out and into the middle of my uterus, exactly where it's meant to be, and then it's done. And I don't want to stand up and leave the room in case it falls out. I desperately need a wee, but oh, I don't want to do one because even though I know the science, I'm so hyper aware of that area that I worry it'll have some negative impact. So instead I lie down in my changing room for ten minutes clutching a crystal – because apparently I'm spiritual and superstitious all of a sudden – and only then, at the risk of a urinary tract infection, I finally (and carefully) go to the loo.

And that was that. The epic embryo transfer. The humongous progress report. The two-fingers up to infertility.

Hey, everyone, listen up. I am PUPO! Yes, I had to google it too – Pregnant Until Proven Otherwise.

Travelling through St Petersburg in a dingy Uber, with the hope of your future child trying to implant in your womb is just magical. I'm not listening to Mr B excitedly rabbiting on, because I am concentrating on every single sensation in my abdomen. I feel like ... like ... I've been *chosen*. Chosen to harbour this little embryo. To protect it whilst it tries to become a person, my person. Oh God, it's nothing short of miraculous. There must be light shining out of me right now, I'm glowing, right? Mr B, am I glowing?

We pull up at our hotel and go straight down for a celebratory dinner, and even though I'm ravenous, I don't think I do anything except giggle. This is the bit that makes me really believe women are fucking incredible. Women of any species – I'm not fussy – but *we* do this! We allow life to happen in our abdominal areas and, as such, I may not be able to toast our impending miracle with a prosecco like the male in this equation, but I don't need bubbles because I am fizzy enough just thinking about it. This is one of those dinners that will be remembered forever. Salty boiled meat with pale potatoes, meaningful conversation and an indescribable gelatinous dessert of some kind.

On our way to the airport the next morning I feel a definite stabbing pain deep in my pelvis somewhere, and I couldn't be happier. This is it! It's trying to implant. Every ounce of research tells me we're in the right time frame; it can feel a bit stabby when the embryo tries to burrow into the uterine lining, which is crazy actually because it's the size of a grain of salt. But it's trying! WOW, look at it go!

When we're on the plane, both beaming with hope and excitement, Mr B tells me the loveliest story ever told. It went like this:

'So, you know the argument we had in the park when Dr Irina told us we could choose the sex of the baby?'

Yes, the lovely story started with an argument, and oh yes, in Russia, you can select the sex of the baby. Oh yes, we were absolutely shocked, too. A little prequel – we arrived in Russia, ridiculous with excitement for our embryo transfer, and while Mr B settled into the hotel sheets, I went through the paperwork we'd need to take into our first meeting with the doctor tomorrow. There was a section in the Paid Medical Services contract that I didn't understand. I'll paraphrase because Russian legalese is even more confounding than British, but essentially, 'Please confirm which gender embryo you would like to transfer.'

Eh? Choose the gender? You can choose the gender? We decided that couldn't possibly be right, we'd leave it blank and double check with Dr Irina when we were scheduled to see her the next day.

Sure enough, the next day she nods and smiles, 'You can choose! Some people prefer to choose, to balance their family.' We knew without conferring that both of our preferences were to *not* choose. That just felt weird, wrong, not natural, too god-like, ew, no way, no thanks. I said, 'Can you please just choose the strongest embryo and transfer that one?' Which was the more polite option.

Dr Irina explains again that because we did the PGD testing, where they analyse the chromosomes and which allows them to even be aware of the gender this early on, that they're all strong, and there's a very equal split between boys and girls. She suggests we take the next hour outside to discuss, before coming back to let her know our decision ahead of the transfer tomorrow.

The moment we get to the incredibly beautiful park and sit on the freezing cold bench to 'discuss', I already know what the conclusion will be. We still won't want to choose. Mr B and I open our mouths at the same time to say the same thing. 'I don't think we should choose,' he says. 'I want a daughter,' I say. Oh! I even surprised myself. Turns out that when given a choice that no one should be allowed to make, I go ahead and subconsciously weigh up my options and make a damn choice. I mean, of course I want a daughter, I'm a woman. One who adores clothes and hoards make-up and drinks Aperol Spritz while gossiping with my girlfriends. Ask most women what their natural inclination would be, and I'd hazzard they'd probably at least be thinking daughter, even if they didn't say it. Same goes for the men wanting sons, I think it's basic biology. Psychology? Whatever, we naturally prefer our own sex. But you wouldn't be asking them before they had to go and tick a box on a contract. That changes everything. That puts so much more weight on the 'inclination' part of the question.

'What?' says Mr B. So I make it worse.

'I don't know, it's just that she asked, so now I'm thinking about it and it's literally my one chance to have a kid, and I just always thought I'd have a daughter.'

'Well, if it's like that, then I want a son,' he says. And then starts making a solid case for his argument, since we're on a tight deadline here. 'I want to take him to Arsenal games.' 'Sons always love their mothers more.' Ooh, that was a sly one. 'Girls are a nightmare when they're teenagers.'

'Well, girls like football too, and you moved out when you were eighteen and I was an angelic teenager, so you're wrong.'

And then we're having an actual full-blown argument, all underpinned by an unease that we're even in a position to be arguing over gender selection. In the end, I give up. 'Why did she have to ask us the stupid question? Why even give us that option? I would have been totally happy with anything, but now it feels like I'm armed with some dangerous power that I don't want to waste.'

Mr B agrees. Of course he does, and we're resolute that we don't want the power to choose, that the doctor should pick by whatever means they usually do, and then not tell us, ever. That horrible hour comprised the kind of ugly conversation you can't ever un-hear, and I feel bad all the way back to the clinic. Really, if I sit with my thoughts, I've got clarity on my actual reasoning for wanting a girl, and it's conflated because of the donor egg situation. This would be my exclusive connection. For my husband, this child will always be a part of him no matter what. I will love and adore it, I know I will, but right now I feel a need for that connection that is only possible between a mother and her daughter. It would be a link unique to me, implicit understanding of each other in a way that the opposite sex can't ever achieve, a really lovely balance to Mr B's genetic advantage. If that sounds selfish, it really isn't. I'm determined to form my own unique bond whichever way this thing goes, but in my heart of hearts, in the darkest depths of shushdom (the place for things that really shouldn't be said out loud), I feel scared that if we have a boy, I'll always be the odd one out.

I tell him all of this but gently and rationally and apologise for fighting. Of course I don't want to choose, we should never have even entertained the idea. I want to approach this like anyone else having a baby: with a thrilling lack of knowledge.

We told Dr Irina to keep it quiet and the rest is recent history.

So, back to the plane.

'I emailed Dr Irina before you went in for the transfer. Here, you can just read it.' He passed his phone to me, and so I read.

Hi Doctor. I am contacting you now in the hope you have not thawed the transfer embryo yet! We wanted a surprise because we did not feel it was right to choose, but I know Sophie has been hoping for a girl, and I think she has been through enough hardship to get where we are today, she deserves a chance for things to finally go her way. If it's not too late, we would like you to please transfer a girl.

If that isn't the most outrageously romantic, unnaturally omniscient gesture, I don't know what is. I cried and hugged him all the way home. Now it's not just a random blastocyst stabbing at my uterine lining. It's my future daughter.

We've made it. The infertility forum milestone that I still can't quite believe I'm experiencing. We are now officially in The Two Week Wait, or '2WW' if we're doing this properly. When I had cancer and was well into my chemotherapy treatment, sometimes I'd catch sight of myself in the mirror and gasp. Oh yeah – that bald, featureless person *is* me. Sometimes I'd forget because much like middle-aged people always feel like they're twenty-six, I felt like me, so I assumed I still looked like me. And then I'd sit on the sofa with my mum and we'd take a moment to go 'What the actual fuck? I'm BALD! From cancer! Isn't that crazy?

This is quite similar actually. I'm in a Two Week Wait. Me! And I have to puncture my own stomach with daily injections, which by the way is one of my proudest achievements.

It's so weird to be hyper aware of your own body. Everything feels very delicate and precarious; I find myself glide-walking, so my motions are smoother than usual. No running down stairs or throwing myself on the sofa, oh no. I even speak in a softer voice, and when Mr B and I get into an (understandably stress-related) argument, I quickly remove myself and sit in the car so my uterus isn't affected. This is how rational The Two Week Wait makes a person.

So what else to expect? For a solid week I've skipped reading my favourite books and watching TV in lieu of focusing on my suspected pregnancy symptoms, so I'm more than qualified to fill you in. Oh my God, my boobs hurt. (Boob, rather. Mastectomy. But when one hurts, the phantom one does too, so we'll stick to plural.) They definitely hurt. And it isn't because I've been poking them, hard, to see if they hurt, it's much more *hormonal*. And all of my friends tell me that they knew they were pregnant because their boobs hurt, so I'm one–nil up. I feel really quite sick actually, very nauseous, but it must be way too early for morning sickness, so I do what every woman in the 2WW knows she shouldn't do, but does. I google it. Google takes me straight to the forums, and there, in the midst of sage advice and abbreviated chatter, every single symptom possible seems to be a sign of pregnancy.

Forum lurking is almost a full-time occupation, because once you've stumbled into Netmums, or Fertility Network, or anyotherIVFforum.com, it's very hard not to dig deeper and deeper. Plus, deciphering some of the abbreviations is like getting quadratic equations when you've joined the class two years later than everyone else. How does everyone else pick it up so seamlessly? Like this:

hopeinheart81: 'So I stupidly tested 9dp5dFET. We had a really good quality 5AA bl, but it was bad news. Has anyone had a bfn from 9dpt and gone on to have a BFP?'

SophieB: 'Eh?'

ICSIbubba: 'Don't give up! One lady on here tested a day early and it was bfn but the next day (on her otd) she got her bfp. She thought she was getting AF! Sending sticky dust.'

They always send sticky dust at the end. It conjures images of those annoying burrs that cling to your cardigan when you go for a walk in the country and then never come off. In this unique language it means 'Hope that the embryo sticks'. To the lining of your womb, rather than your cardigan, but I was on the right lines. So you see, with all the googling, researching, language learning and then desperately searching and searching until you find the success story that matches your symptoms – because there always is one – it's quite time consuming.

It's also very easy to send you into a tailspin. Last night, for instance, I was up until two in the morning, tears glinting in the eerie blue glow of the laptop screen. Because I have all these exciting symptoms of pregnancy according to everyone (kind of) on here (OK, some people on here). But I also have headaches. And no one seems to list headaches as an early symptom of a 7dp5dFET that led to a BFP. Oh sorry, I lost myself there. They don't seem to be a symptom seven days after a Frozen Embryo Transfer using a five-day-old blastocyst – which is where I am right now – that then led to a Big Fat Positive. Whole new language. Quite a confounding one too.

In fact, one woman from the depths of the internet had a negative result after experiencing headaches, so I'm sure now that I will go the same way. The only thing that will allow me to shut this laptop and go to sleep is more searching and searching until I find what I'm looking for. Searching ... searching ... rephrasing my search terms in case that brings up something diff— aha! There it is:

> Bunnyhop19: 'I am D10PT [day 10 post transfer] and over the past couple of days have started getting a headache – very similar to what I get before AF. [Aunt Flo, aka your period, duh.] Was convinced it was all over for me but I just POAS [peed on a stick] and it's BFP.' [You already know that one. Oh you don't? My bad, it's Big Fat Positive.]

Ahhnd breathe. It may be four in the morning, but at least I'm now safe in the knowledge that there's a tiny chance insomnia is a symptom of forum lurker neurosis. Everybody knows googling is never a reliable source of truth-dom when it comes to anything medical. As a cancer survivor I am well versed in this, trust me. I don't know why I let my resolve slip when it comes to The Two Week Wait, but I obviously need some positive affirmation right now. Man, this is anticipatory anxiety on a whole other level. The only real truth comes from the nurse at the fertility clinic when I call in a state the next morning. 'Well, the hormone injections you're taking mimic early pregnancy symptoms so get off the forums. You can't know in the two weeks whether it's the progesterone or pregnancy. Just wait until your official blood test next week.'

An entire tortuous week left to go and no alcohol allowed to help me through it. What fresh hell is this?

The night before my official test date, I caved and peed on a stick. I managed to get to now, to middle age, before I ever had the need to take a pregnancy test. No irresponsible teenage shenanigans in my back catalogue. So this feels strangely thrilling for more reasons than the most pressing one here. I've only ever seen it done dramatically on TV, so peeing on a stick for the first time feels like I'm in my own film. Rooting for the protagonist in this instance, rather than hoping she's not pregnant so her husband doesn't have to bring up a child he will never know is not his own. My own plot builds momentum as I save up my wee to make sure I have maximum output, and then, huh, turns out I pee sideways – who knew – so when I return from the bathroom and hand it to Mr B, the whole stick is sodden. This doesn't feel as romantic as I'd hoped. The two minutes waiting for a pregnancy test result to materialise do not conform to the usual rules of time passing. This wait is interminably long, and after approximately fifteen seconds I start seriously worrying about it being negative. I feel self-conscious, embarrassed, ashamed. I can't look at Mr B, I start crying, oh my God this is a bit over the top. Is it the hormones, am I pregnant? What if I'm pregnant!

Is it time? Is it time? Now, is it time?

I so wish I could do this part solo. No offence to Mr B, it's a Scorpio quirk I have. I prefer to do things quietly on my own. And then I go TA DA, I just did that. Like when I took my driving test without telling a soul. Or even earlier, when I learnt to swim without my armbands (future baby, do NOT do that on your own. Your mother needs to be there). This personality trait is not useful now, when it seems the events of the last year or so are all culminating in the worst-ever scenario, where I just don't want to have to let someone I love down so badly, at the same time as me, and oh fuck the time is up. I can't look. But this embryo is his potential daughter as much as she is mine, so I can't run away from Mr B and process the result on my own either. I turn the stick over …

Looks like she didn't make it. I wish I'd never known that it was a girl that was trying to embed in my stupid uterus. That she was going to be a she. I think it hurts even more.

4.

How do you deal with a negative pregnancy result?

NOT PREGNANT

The stick I peed on two minutes ago is shouting at me. I'm immediately heartbroken and it's the physically painful kind that makes your insides twist and, oh, ow, there's abject disappointment too. Disappointment in this negative result when I foolishly let myself believe it would be positive. In my hopes for our immediate future, in the wasted gargantuan effort to go all the way to bloody Russia to try to get pregnant and, most of all, in myself, for failing to get pregnant. But at the same time, I had kind of expected it not to go our way because, sadly, over the last few years this is my standpoint and I'm subconsciously sticking to it. Hope is dangerous, if you ask me.

I don't think I'd be crying quite so hard if Mr B wasn't cuddling me and telling me it was OK, we'd try again. Because he should be just as sad too – he must be – but he's comforting me instead. I think this is how we've evolved in our tough-luck relationship. We take it in turns to be desolate, so one can pick the other back up and then, whup! Your turn.

So I know we're both in this crappy boat, but I am also aware that I'm dealing with some feelings that he *can't* be having. I recognise that already, even while I'm clutching this stupid pee stick. I'm irrationally humiliated, full of self-loathing, in total disbelief that I, a verified over-achiever, have failed, devastated about my illness breaking my body in this extra way. And very worried that I won't be able to carry a baby at all, ever. So I try really hard not to feel these things. This is how I'd like to deal with this particular bad news, please. I'd like to not feel it. And the only way to do that, I think, is to retain a morsel of hope.

Maybe this stick is lying. Maybe I didn't pee on it correctly – it was a distinctly sideways wee after all. The forums do all say it's possible to have a negative home test and then a surprise positive when you go for the official blood test result. Maybe my hCG hormone levels (produced by the cells surrounding a growing embryo) are a bit too low for this crappy over-the-counter pregnancy test to read. And actually, the Russian clinic also told me to test on day 11, so *surely* that's too early, because otherwise it would be called the 11-day wait rather than the traditional 14. Oh, OK, wait. There's a bit of light peeking through. This might not be over for me just yet. I can feel the feelings backing off a little as I start to calm down and foolishly, or otherwise, pin every hope for mine and Mr B's future happiness on a date with a blood test tomorrow. Right now, it may not seem like the greatest of ideas, but it's the only one that is going to enable me to get on with my evening and feel OK enough to eat some food and look my husband in the eye again. Good bargaining with you, my own mind, now switch off for a bit, yeah?

The reason they do an official blood test – known as the Beta test – is to take a measure that will accurately indicate the level of hCG hormone in your blood, and then use it as a benchmark to make sure an early pregnancy is developing as it should. And this is precisely why I still have hope in my heart as I get the train to central London and slowly walk down the street to the clinic where my blood will be taken and the result delivered back to me four or so hours later. It's the only way to get an accurate result, and my emotionally damaged logic tells me this is because all other tests must be inaccurate. Ergo, yesterday's negative result is unlikely to be true. Because I really do *feel* like I'm pregnant. And isn't that what everyone says? That they just knew?

The blood clinic is great and the test is quick and then I'm nudged out the door and back to waiting. The last part of this tortuous two weeks of waiting that isn't technically two weeks (but I appreciate the alliteration works better).

I'm to get my results by email or text message from Mr Hiyer's clinical nurse Laura. This adds to the anticipatory terror, because it means now my phone is my enemy. I *hate* waiting for results. Especially life-changing ones – because of the cancer connotations – but I'm trying to separate out the anxiety and recognise this as being at the total other end of the spectrum. Whereas during my cancer scans I'd be desperately hoping for a normal outcome over a devastatingly bad one, now I'm dreading normal and hoping for joy of all joys. So, it's win-win, right? Except it does not feel like it. By my calculations it should be around midday that I get the news, and I make it to eleven-thirty just fine. The last half hour is a jittery blur of constant email refreshing and phone battery level checking. Refreshing, checking. Refreshing, checking. Until it comes.

Subject: Results for SOPHIE BERESINER, requested by HIYER

shudders
opens email

Hi Sophie
I'm sorry it is a negative result. Give us a call tomorrow if you want to talk anything through.

Just like that. Did I mention it's my birthday today? At least I can have a fucking glass of fucking champagne now.

That's how I plan on dealing with this particular negative pregnancy test result.

Unfortunately, a definitive answer means dealing with definitive feelings. As much as I'd prefer to skip this part, the emotional impact of the last couple of months – all the effort and discomfort and money and hope that went into them – is quite overwhelming, and so it's absolutely impossible. If I try to break it down, maybe it will help. So here goes:

Shame

My emotional response starts with and centres around shame. I feel ashamed of myself. I couldn't do it, I got it wrong. This is literally what my species are built to do. Women everywhere manage to have babies, even crack-addled ones. Even clinically ill people or one-night-stand participants, but I couldn't do it even with a lot of medical intervention to help. It feels like my bike has been fitted with stabilisers and I still fell off it. In front of an audience of everyone I've told about our plans. How shameful is that? It's irrational, of course it is, but it smacks you round the face nevertheless. And it's partly why I keep apologising to Mr B. I know I don't need to, and he doesn't blame me, but I keep doing it anyway. That will be down to the next feeling …

Guilt

My husband did not sign up for this. I recognised the inappropriateness of what I was about to say as soon as it formed in my head, but it forced its way through until it was sitting on my tongue waiting for me to stop crying and give it some airtime. 'You can go and find someone healthy to have a baby with if you want to. I mean you have a chance, this is your opportunity. I wouldn't blame you.' What I was inferring sounds ridiculous out loud, but I'm doing the classic manoeuvre. Testing the limits, pushing painful buttons, and reminding him that whilst I am stuck like this forever, he could in fact go forth and procreate. The very best that I can offer him is a baby that shares his DNA with a total stranger. And now I've downgraded to no baby at all. It's not fair on either of us and man, I feel *so* guilty. Also, I absolutely know he won't leave me – we had the same conversation when I was bald and useless and extra-high maintenance – so I obviously said it to get myself some sympathy and reassurance. So great, now I feel selfish too.

Pride

I've come to suspect there are always positives to be found in every situation, but sometimes you have to look really hard. Like with chemotherapy, for instance, losing all my hair meant no need for waxing. I could wear a skirt in summer at the blink of an eye. Bikini ready at all times. It was frankly amazing. But I digress; I realise from all that has led to this particular experience that I *can* be as strong as people tell me I am, and I can deal with things that most people shouldn't have to. For every, 'I don't know how you do it,' I can only offer a 'neither the hell do I.' But I do do it, and if I sit and think about that, I definitely feel some swagger mixed in there somewhere.

Self pity

WHY ME? No, seriously, why me? I'm quite certain that upon balance breast cancer at age thirty, a mastectomy, dead ovaries and the requirement of donor eggs was more than enough of a fair share for me, thank you. So come on, really. Why couldn't this have gone my way? Because it would have pretty much fixed all of the above. I would love for there to be a time when I don't have to feel sorry for myself – it's very solipsistic and I'm not really into that.

Anger

Fuck this shit.

Panic

This is definitely not how my life was supposed to go. What if this first round of IVF failing means there's something fundamentally wrong with my body (understandably, it's been through quite a lot) and it won't ever work? That makes perfect sense to me. What if it not working is the universe trying to tell me something, namely that I'm not supposed to be a mother? I'm not supposed to be a mother. I'm just throwing money and time and agonising effort at something that is just not going to happen for me.

Resolve

Actually no, I refuse to take no for an answer. I can do this. I know I need to be a mother. I can't imagine my life, my home, without a child in it, so I simply won't allow that to happen. Giving up hasn't ever really been an option, otherwise I would have done it ages ago. So I'm hoicking up my socks and I'm going to feel better so I can be better. Do better. Because it does seem to be down to me …

Angst

Yes, that. Generalised, daily, anticipatory, retrospective, any brand of angst will do because it's very adaptable that one, lends itself brilliantly to every part of this experience. It's the *pressure* because, ultimately, as much as Mr B reassures me that I don't need to feel half the things on this list, I am the one who needs her body to start working in the way it's supposed to work. It's me who needs to maintain and administer the right treatment protocol, to inject myself – correctly – in the stomach, to get myself to the clinic at the right times over and over again and have the invasive scans and collect the right results. I need to have my uterus achieve optimum thickness, please, I need to research all the complementary therapies I can be doing or taking or actualising to better my chances of success. I need to eat healthy and get acupuncture and avoid coffee and alcohol and all the other exact things I'm craving because of all the guilt and shame and panic and angst. So yes. It's quite stressful, this.

The only real way I know how to feel better about anything is to bury the pain and move on as quickly as possible. My prescription for dealing with grief is 'replace it'. If it's death we're talking about, it only works for pets, not people, but honestly, there's nothing better for healing a broken heart than a new kitten to get to know and fall in love with. If it sounds desperate, it probably is, but if I ever have to lose one, my heart hurts too much to risk fully exploring that pain. I'm kind of doing the same thing here, with my fertility. Grieving the loss of my own eggs? QUICK, replace them with somebody else's! Get on a plane to Russia, do not pass go. So, the only thing for right now has got to be picking myself up and planning the next cycle.

Right, it's been quite long enough to process this bad news. I am in contact with Mr Hiyer and Dr Irina within an hour of my negative result, telling them my plan rather than asking for theirs:

> Emotionally, I am ready to start again immediately. I have the medication here, I just need the treatment plan from you. I would feel much better if we did not have to wait too much.
>
> **P.S.** Is there a protocol to try something different on the 2nd attempt?

P.P.S. Any ideas as to why it didn't implant? I had a bit of a stomach ache the next day, could that be a contributor?

And so we started again, the following week in fact. Boom! Clinic, scans, medicine, scans, injections, scans, visa, plane, Russia, plane, home. This time my official test date would be my favourite of all days: Christmas Day. A positive sign? A Christmas miracle? The best present a girl could ever ask for?

Nope. Not today caller. But hey, at least I could have a Christmas champagne, eh?

The bigger blow comes from knowing how much more we put into that second try, that tells us how much we have to put into the next one. This must be something akin to walking out the prison exit only to be told you need to serve another few months. That's how long it takes to have a rest, re-plan, do the medical cycle, arrange the logistics, the travel, muster the new hope and enthusiasm. But what else can we do? We swallow it, we muster the beginnings of hope and, a month or so later, we start again, again.

This time Mr B was denied a visa. 'You were what?' I cried, literally. 'I've been too many times in a year. Apparently three is maximum for a tourist visa.' So what the absolute hell does this mean for me? It means I have to jump through hoops and go around the houses and add another degree of uncertainty to the uncertainty pile

I'm currently balancing precariously on the very top of. After acquiring a letter from Dr Irina and putting a very heartfelt personal note in with my application, my passport was stamped and I was on my way. Thank you, higher embassy powers. So now I may have to go to Russia to get impregnated on my own, but at least I'm managing to go at all.

Needless to say it felt very different this time. I'm scared and hopeful and so far out of my comfort zone I feel like I'm on another planet. It's so isolating being solo in a foreign country when not only can you not speak the language, you can't even read a sign to vaguely guess what it's indicating. I vow to decipher the Russian alphabet as my payback for getting pregnant in this beautiful country, but until then I hole up in my hotel and eat from the room service menu until it's time for me to book an Uber to my third (and please, PLEASE, final) embryo transfer.

Back home in the background, Mr Hiyer has been getting a little concerned at the repeated failures. He would have hoped for some good news for me by now because we've done a lot of best-chance-for-success legwork. We did the biopsies on the embryos, so we know they're chromosomally perfect, grade A, top of the range, so it's not their fault. He performed a hysteroscopy on my uterus to do a full survey of their new home before they could move in, and you know what? My uterus is about as perfect and inviting as it's possible for a uterus to be. I am inordinately proud of that. We are doing the gold standard of treatment protocols. I'm having acupuncture with a renowned fertility acupuncturist called Emma Cannon who, according to the man himself, makes Mr Hiyer's success rates soar, so what is it? What's the problem? IVF is never an exact science, but because Mr Hiyer doesn't know the Russian clinic or lab, he'd have felt much more comfortable if we could've brought the embryos to London and have him perform the transfers. There is a very cynical part of me, the control freak part, that suddenly realises we have no proof that PGD even happened. I mean, I don't know how I'd have actual proof from anywhere, unless I watched the lab perform the tests, but all I know is I paid £9k into a Russian bank account, and then I got an email saying six of them were good and the others were no good. What if it's all a massive racket and they don't even do the testing? What if the embryos aren't embedding because they're not good quality? What if I'm utterly paranoid, potentially from all the hormones I'm taking, but still? What if?

Mr Hiyer suggests we look into the logistics around bringing the embryos here, to a lab that he knows, and letting him take over the entirety of my care. I'm hoping after this go, this solo venture (superstitious me likes that there is a different variable this time, it must mean it's going to work), that I won't need to think about shipping embryos across an ocean. At least until we start to plan for baby number two.

Now is definitely not the time to think about that because here I am again. In my surgical gown, maniacally rubbing some amethyst with my thumb for good luck, and waiting for Dr Irina to come and collect me. Only apparently she's away right now, so it's her colleague Dr Alexi who comes instead. I refuse to panic about this. I only have emotional capacity for one unsettling turn of events, and the absence of my husband ticks that box. So I pretend to myself that I'm totally cool with the whole thing as I follow him down the corridor into the surgical suite. His English is not as good as Dr Irina's, so other than a perfunctory, 'Hello, I'm Dr Alexi, and you are Sophie,' *nods*, we haven't really chatted much. Whilst we walk single file to the transfer room he turns round to start up a conversation:

'This time I put in boy.'

Oh, for fuck's sake Dr Alexi, I didn't want to know! I *so* didn't want to know. I told everyone after the first time – when I kept imagining my embryo as a daughter – that I didn't ever want to know. It seems Dr Alexi didn't get the memo, and now I can't unknow it, so I just nod and smile. He can't read a room, this guy. He continues, 'Only boys now. All embryos boys.'

Eh? No, no that's not correct. Because Dr Irina told us there was a perfectly even split just before the first transfer. She was lying?

'All boys,' he confirms. So, she was lying. This is a lot of information to take in on this very short walk to the surgical suite. I'm trying desperately to compartmentalise. All boys then. OK. But, argh Why? Why tell me this Dr Alexi? I did not ask for this highly sensitive information. As it is, after two negative results, I'd be overjoyed if I fell pregnant with a shoe right now, but it's still a shock and, right now, when I should be focusing on feeling harmonious and calm, I'm scrabbling with feelings about my future. So I'll never have a daughter. Ever, then. Please God let me love and nurture this little boy, who has just been defrosted in the embryology lab next door, but then what about the next child? I already know it won't be a daughter. How dare this strange man have taken that unknown away from me. I did not want to know!

Of course when I came out of the transfer, I was convinced this poor kid didn't even stand a chance. I was so screwed up with negative energy and inappropriate disappointment the whole time, that this little embryo would get one whiff and not even try to implant. I'd fucked it up again. Thank you, Dr Alexi.

So, yeah. It was a massive shock when eleven days later my blood test came back positive. Uh huh. *Pos-i-TIVE!*

It worked! It worked, it worked, it worked, IT WORKED. This time I didn't get an impersonal email or text message. Laura from Mr Hiyer's office called me, her voice wobbling with anticipatory excitement.

'Sophie. You're pregnant!' instead of the more traditional, 'Hello.'

I was at work, so I really needed to contain my excitement. Actually, I really needed to not be at work, I needed to be with Mr B, jumping (gently) for joy and toasting ourselves with (non-alcoholic) prosecco. Instead, I went and sat in the stairwell and called him, shaking.

'It worked!' I said, instead of 'Hello.' He didn't say anything.

'Hello?' Nothing

'Babe? Are you there?'

He was crying so he couldn't get any words out. And then he didn't believe me until he almost did. And after clarifying and clarifying, he really did and he was still speechless. And then he had to go because he had a meeting but woah, this is what pure happiness feels like. Who knew?

I called my mum and dad, who immediately made a plan to take us out for dinner that night to celebrate. This! This is what I've been waiting for. This pure, unadulterated joy and success, shared with the people I love the most, who helped me wherever and whenever they could. This is even better because it's for everyone. My body outdid itself. It did what I had begged it to do, over and over again, and now I feel absolutely miraculous. This incomparable feeling that I can't even explain. As if I have the world's most beautiful secret inside me, and I can feel it bubbling up to the surface, like that kid-before-Christmas fizzy elation. It's pure love. I need to go and tell everyone I love how much I love them. For now, Mr B and my parents will have to do.

We go to a lovely local restaurant and extract untold amounts of joy from considering what I'm not allowed to eat on the menu. My dad enlists the help of the waitress. 'My daughter just found out she's pregnant, so please don't let her order the Camembert. What else can't she have?'

We toast with prosecco – I have one sip and then pour the rest into Mr B's glass, and we plan the big party my dad wants to throw when the baby comes. It's a huge relief, it's a massive soothing resolution to the entirety of the last six shitty, scary years. For all four of us, really. God this feels amazing.

Mr B has to go away again. His job is quickly becoming one that takes him away to various parts of Europe on a pretty regular basis. So he leaves me, he tries to concentrate on what he has to do, while I do the same back home. In this case, it's harbouring my precious secret and letting it make every moment of every day so much more exciting and special, for both of us. And then, one day while I've popped out of work to grab lunch with my friend, I get a voicemail from Mr Hiyer asking me to call him back. I always do this with doctors, I hold my breath and let the room spin before I manage to get myself somewhere private and make the call. I hate getting these kinds of messages because it's impossible not to dial back with shaky fingers, feeling anxiety settle into my jawbone, knowing they have something medically important to tell me. But I remind myself this is a positive medical experience, it's not cancer.

When I hear him greet me on the phone, I know it's bad news even before he says it. 'I'm so sorry Sophie, your hCG levels aren't rising at the rate we would like them to. It indicates a non-viable pregnancy, but let's do another test in a few days to see where we are.'

I decide not to tell my husband until we do actually know where we are. He doesn't need this uncertainty while he's away from home because, and I don't know if I'm being desperately naive here, there's still a chance, isn't there? Otherwise, why would we do another test at all?

A few days later I'm back in a dark hole, with a confirmation that this pregnancy will not progress, and I'm wondering how many knocks I can take before I break in half. I don't know how I'm going to break it to Mr B, who is due back from this trip very late tonight. I can't bear the thought of delivering this news, of breaking his heart, and so I just don't think. I get in bed and I stay there, curled under the duvet, until he creeps in hours later. He knows just by looking at me, so that I don't even have to clarify his worst fears, but I say it anyway. 'I'm sorry, I'm not pregnant anymore.'

It takes me the usual three days of bargaining with myself before I'm over it (over it, ha! I buried it) and ready for round four. Time is running out, I need to ease the pain of this battle by winning the war, so Mr Hiyer and I make plans to bring the remaining embryos back to England for him to perform the transfers. It's a delicate situation. I don't want to risk suggesting we are unhappy with our treatment in Russia – no one wants to upset the balance in this scenario – so I appeal to the lovely staff and explain it is more and more difficult to keep getting visas, and the travel is taking its toll. They absolutely agree to cooperate and we put everything in motion. The complexity of this situation lies in the difference in the laws between our two countries. In Russia our egg donation agreement was anonymous. Our donor wanted to retain her anonymity, and we did not need to know who she was. In the UK, every donor needs to join a register in order to be identifiable to the child if he or she wishes to know his or her genetic background. Obviously, these are not compatible stances, but if the donor agreed to be identified on the British registry, and all the paperwork was in order, we could still transport the embryos.

I won't go into the depths of the details because I'm still somewhat confused about them myself, but there was an unfortunate admin error on the Russian side. A big one, huge. They sent all the documents to the official UK body in charge of accepting biomaterial from another country, including the passport scan of the donor, and they cc'd me in. Thereby making the donor no longer anonymous, without her consent. I didn't look. I know that sounds suspicious, but I didn't want to. I don't actually want to see a photo of the woman who has effectively replaced me in this pivotal genetic role. What if it burns into my retina and then materialises every time I look at my baby? Dramatic, yes, but also neurotically true. But it was there, in my inbox for me to look at nonetheless and so, just like that, all the parameters suddenly changed.

Red flags popped up everywhere, the whole thing fell apart, and Mr Hiyer informed me that if we pushed it, our embryos could be blacklisted from the UK forever. It's like a biomaterial mafia. You don't mess with this system, and an admin error of this magnitude is definitely messing.

I sent an email to Creation Clinic gently suggesting it was a shame that they fucked up so monumentally, and was there anything at all they could do? I didn't receive one back. Instead, when I went for my fourth embryo transfer, I was not picked up from the airport. Unusual! We had been met at arrivals by a lovely driver every time before, so we never had any difficulty getting to the hotel and then the clinic for the transfer. Mr B was obviously visa-less, so at home, and I, after searching the entire terminal for about an hour, tentatively made my own confused way.

Still, must be another admin error, they do have previous on that front. Maybe they thought I was on a different flight ...

When I arrived for my transfer appointment the next day, I followed the usual protocol and went first to pay for the procedure. When the receptionist wordlessly passed me the bill, I pointed out another error. Come on guys, repeated errors are not exactly conducive to confidence, here. The fee was almost double what I paid the last three times. I pushed the bill back, she made a hushed phone call (not that I would have been able to understand a word of it anyway), and then she replaced the receiver, looked at me and said, 'Today, price changed.' I explained that it can't have almost doubled, and I can't only just be hearing about it on the morning of my transfer, please call again and make sure they know there is an error. She looked at me impassively, and said, 'You want procedure or not?'

Ah. I see. I paid. I understood. I should have learnt from the Dr Sokolov experience; it's not wise to send an email complaint to the people who are holding your entire future in their surgically gloved hands. At this point, they could be planning to transfer a droplet of water into my uterus for all I knew. Needless to say, transfer number four didn't work either.

You'd think that with this much practice at something, I'd get better at it, but that rule doesn't apply to me and my Two Week Waiting. Every time I enter that all-too familiar obsessive-introspection phase, I feel worse. More panicky, more frightened of the hope – because the higher you climb, the further you fall – but hopeful nonetheless. More afraid of going to the loo in case there is blood in my knickers. More obsessively checking the forums (why do you keep doing this to yourself, Sophie?) to ascertain what the colour of the blood means. Maybe pink is a good sign or if it's brown, is it bad? Every day of accumulative anticipation is more stressful, to the point when I wonder if my body must feel like a hostile environment for the little guys. No wonder it's not working. And then I start preparing myself for the next round and it's the only thing that makes me feel better. And worse. Argh.

Because I know this has to be the last one. I know my body is going through the mill at as fast a rate as possible because I have to get back on the medication that is keeping my threat of recurring cancer at bay, and I'm just waiting for the phonecall from my team at The Royal Marsden to tell me it's time to stop.

My choices now are give up or go back to Creation Clinic for this fifth and final embryo transfer. It's not really a choice because I just can't stop. Otherwise this whole emotional debacle will have been for nothing; I don't know how I would ever be able to spend comfortable, peaceful time with myself again. So I'm trying to muster some enthusiasm and hope for round five, but it's bloody hard when you're in an unsuccessful IVF holding pattern. I'm already one of those sad stories of repeated unexplained failures, but hold up. Maybe I can be the 'it worked on her fifth round!' happy ending that gives other non-starters a bit of hope. The miraculous last chance story of belief, endurance and ultimately, joy. I could do with some of that right now. As I'm packing for my eighth trip to Russia in a year, I remember to transfer extra funds into 'Baby Bank Account'. Who the hell knows what direction it's going to go in this time.

As it happens, everything went very nice and politely. It was as if the previous transfer experience was a blip that we didn't ever need to speak of again. Dr Irina earnestly wished me all the luck in the world as she packed me back off to England, and on the way home I said a silent prayer to whatever higher power might represent the infertility shares. As I looked out of the window at the city of St Petersburg getting smaller and smaller, I begged my future son to settle in. Please, please let this one stick. Please don't make me have to do surrogacy. I want to carry my own child. I don't want to have to rely on a stranger to have that experience for me. I don't want to have to live in a strange country on my own for weeks or months waiting for the birth of my baby and then waiting to be able to bring it home. PLEASE.

You know what? Those higher powers might have been listening. On the last chance. At the exact peak of email inbox refreshing, when I decided my racing heart was about to pack up, and this regular spike of extreme anxiety would absolutely kill me, let alone any baby, I got a text message from Laura:

YOU ARE PREGNANT.

Are you sure?

Because so far, nothing has ever been sure, before.

Yes! It's happening. Go celebrate.

Oh my God, the wave of this I-don't-know-what emotion is like medicine. It feels like I can breathe again; it was supposed to take this long so I'd appreciate it all the more.

Mr B is due to arrive home from a work trip in the early hours of the morning. I haven't been able to stop thinking about him throughout this last desperate attempt. It's an awkward mixture of not wanting to let him down, again, because, try as I might, it is my body that keeps failing us, so I can't help but suffer the burden of guilt here. But also love, compassion, empathy for this man in my life who is wading through thigh-high quicksand right along with me. I know how he is feeling because I am feeling it too, and I wouldn't wish that on anyone, let alone the closest person to me. Poor Mr B. Away from home, from me, from the end of this last Two Week Wait. It must be a blessed relief for him, too, but that feeling will be way too deep down to access, if I know my husband at all. It'll be buried beneath tonnes of worry, anxiety, homesickness. And he's been plastering a professional smile on his face throughout, because work doesn't stop just because we're both dying inside. He's been FaceTiming me every evening and I almost wish he wouldn't because watching his sad, tired face on my phone screen is depressing both of us. He didn't think it would happen. I didn't think it would happen, and now look! It's only gone and bloody happened! And I have a joyous plan.

I peed on a stick. And even though Laura has already told me I'm pregnant, I spend the next two minutes with my heart in my mouth. I've been here too many times before. This stupid bit of plastic represents everything that is wrong with the world, to me, but oh! Laura was

71

right! I feel the warm glow of ecstatic relief when the two lines appear. I am on my own at home, but I'm grinning like a maniacal clown. God, this feeling is incredible, only heightened by the tickly anticipation of Mr B getting home, finding this little bit of stupid plastic in a gift box on his pillow.

He didn't get back until one in the morning, and I pretended to be asleep as he wearily crept in and took off his travel clothes. 'Hi babe,' I mumbled, faux-sleepily, as I turned over to see him find his present. I will never forget the look on his face then: a kind of deflated exhausted, because good grief this process takes its toll. I know this always affects him, even when he's pretending otherwise, in different ways to me, and sometimes the exact same ways, but constant disappointment is hard to recover from. Also, he knows the results are imminent, but I haven't told him exactly when because, truth be told, I can't stand the self-imposed pressure from anyone anymore, even my own husband. This, though. This divine opportunity to deliver the news we have been working so hard towards, in this lovely way. This makes it all worthwhile.

'What's this?' he says as he flops on the bed and picks up the box. I tell him it's just a silly present and watch as he unties the ribbon, opens the box and stares, uncomprehending, for about ten slow seconds.

Then he bawled like a baby. Apt, that.

*   *   *

We were tentatively ecstatic for the next couple of weeks, aware, as always, that things have gone wrong before. But I was quietly confident in the universe this time, in fate, in the fact that this is the kind of happy ending you read about in books. It's our last go, the ultimate save! So it's extra amazing that it's all going to work out for us, at last.

And then my hormone levels stopped rising. And I knew I had lost the last pregnancy before the repeated blood tests told us so. Later, I called my mum to tell her the news. I actually apologised, quietly, and then I hung up, not feeling worthy to deal with the certain sympathy that would follow.

So this is it, the end of the line. I can't believe it. I'm that person who aimlessly kept scrambling around to find a bit more money to just do it once more, and kept going and kept going until I'm just a sad minority statistic. When The Royal Marsden call me to banish the idea of any more IVF, it's like an intervention. I was in an addictive cycle and I probably would have kept going and going until my body gave up. But all the while, festering in the background, was this extreme neuroses of not being on my cancer medication. I was actually taking high levels of the very hormone that my post-cancer drugs work to suppress. How's that for a hypochondriac's year-and-a-half-long worst nightmare? So now the decision has been taken out of my hands. I have to stop and it is a relief and an atrocity at the same time.

But I can't give up. So, what now?

5.

How does surrogacy work, exactly?

Well, I don't know, I haven't particularly had to think about it until now. Except from afar, with fond interest and intrigue in Elton John – who I adore by the way – he and David have such lovely sons! And obviously Kim Kardashian, who I'm less fond of but yes, has also done it. I suspect the likes of Elton and Kim K can't teach me too much about how it works in the real world, because celebrity surrogacy cannot possibly exist on the same financial or logistical plane as citizen surrogacy, and the latter is what I'm currently looking at. With my shoulders slumped, back in Mr Hiyer's office to discuss my options.

It's not the surrogacy step that's making me so slouchy. On the contrary, I surprised myself by fully embracing the idea at first thought. Mr B and I were on the way back from a weekend wedding and we had a short conversation about what we'd do now my attempts at donor egg IVF were done, over, closed for business. It was only short because it was very obvious. There is just no question we'll be giving up. Our child was not supposed to come to us that way, so, fine, it will be another. And if the other is surrogacy, then bring it. Five rounds of IVF took a toll on my body and my wildly undulating stress levels, so I think I'm OK about not doing that part anymore. The thought of surrogacy – of having to not only bring someone in to replace the egg donation part of my role, but now the pregnancy part too – actually feels … calming. It feels *right*, like things are finally slotting into place. Like I said, I'm surprised at myself.

So how do we actually make it happen? That's where we need quite a bit of guidance, so the obvious first stop is the office of the one doctor I trust. It's true that we didn't achieve the result we'd hoped for under his care, but I don't blame him for a second. There's no knowing with assisted baby making. It could be me, it could be Russia, it could be him, but there's zero point in dwelling. I trust him because he made me feel calm and cared for, and so listening to him now I hoover up his sage advice and, well, I'm a bit overwhelmed by it.

Surrogacy in the UK works like one of those infographic quizzes that takes you to the outcome that best applies to you. First question. Do you have a friend or relative who will act as your surrogate and carry your baby? 'Yes'! Get that person to Mr Hiyer's office for a suitability scan and hope you can move forward. Acquire new donor eggs (requires its own infographic quiz), get cracking, have baby, be forever in grateful debt to that amazing friend or family member.

Or, like me, was your first answer 'No'? Find a stranger surrogate. Hmm, OKaaay.

Second question: Do you have more time or do you have more money?

If it's money, then it might make more sense to go elsewhere, take the Elton John/Kim K path of least resistance, but we'll come back to that.

If it's time, you could join a specialised not-for-profit organisation like Surrogacy UK, and then consider how many people without a kindly friend or relative will also be looking for a stranger-surrogate in the UK. It's hard to get proper figures on this, but when I researched it once before there were around thirty-five known surrogates in the UK. So now consider how you become the one to get matched with a member of this very, very rare breed. What you generally do is go to what is essentially a 'mixer' event. You are invited to an organised social with many other hopeful infertiles, you get dressed in whatever it is that you consider the most appealing to a stranger-surrogate, and then you battle everyone else for their affections. It's like surrogate *Hunger Games*, but infinitely less violent. How far will you go to undercut the other seventeen people interested in Angie from Newcastle? Will you enlist your husband? Send him to the bar to have a friendly chat with the other husbands to garner vital information? How can anyone possibly be themselves at those things? The very thought of this kind of forced fun, with so much pressure hanging over you all along with the bunting, fills me with horror. With horror! I can't do that. I don't want to do that. I'm not even speaking from experience here because I didn't do that.

But we'll get to that too.

First of all, this is how it works legally and logistically. There are two types of surrogacy: traditional and gestational. Traditional is when a supremely altruistic person carries a baby made from *her own eggs* and – if we're talking in the context of me here – Mr B's sperm. If that sets alarm bells ringing, you're right. It's a worry and it's quite rare, precisely because it's quite worrying. Most of the moral and ethical questions that surrogacy gives rise to centre on the surrogate's relationship with the baby; her bond, how she will feel giving up a child she carried for nine months et cetera. You can see that giving birth to, and then giving up, a baby that is genetically related to her might make things decidedly more complex. For 'complex' read 'harrowing'. We will definitely not be going down this route and, to be honest, I'm not even sure how we would go about it if we wanted to. Other people seem to have a clue though, when I float the idea of surrogacy to them. A wry smile. A slap on Mr B's back. Um, no you misogynistic morons, the father will not be fornicating with Angie from Newcastle.

The other more common kind is gestational surrogacy, when a supremely altruistic person carries a baby that is no genetic relation to her, be it made from the intended mother's egg and her husband's sperm, or someone else's egg and my husband's sperm, aka, my way.

So now that we have that cleared up, there is the big, huge, overwhelming question of why? Why would we take this huge and still quite unusual leap? There is a definite argument, which again, we'll get to, for giving a home to a child in need who already exists in the world. But the thing is, our path seems to have been trying to approximate the one I should have taken, had cancer not dug it out and built a massive obstruction there instead. So we're over here, trying to pick up the pieces. Once we've postulated and percolated, surrogacy represents something really quite special for us. Here is why:

There are huge pros, starting with the biggest – this is Mr B's last chance to have his own child. In my mind it is not necessary for a father to be genetically related to his kid (or a mother, obviously, otherwise what am I even doing here?) but it's evidently preferable, for us at least (otherwise, again, what am I even doing here? And why does IVF even exist? Or surrogacy for that matter?). Especially, when you consider the biology and psychology of mankind. The 'man' part, specifically. Man's primary urge is to procreate. It is what guides him in choosing a mate. When Mr B chose me, I appeared, at first glance, gloriously fertile. Not too pale, not too skinny, decent hips, glowing in the right places at the right time of the month, lustrous hair etc. I was healthy, and his primal radar sought that out, and identified me as fit for purpose. Romantic, eh? This is a great argument for clarifying that at their core, men are in fact as basic as we often imagine. Sorry men, it's biology, and you can't fight science.

So there it is, I may not be able to have my own genetic child, and I'm OK with that because I know I'll be a mother to anything that needs me, but my husband can.

He would equally be excellent at fathering whoever needed him, but that could still be his own child, and I would be over the moon to meet that little person. It would go some way to helping me too.

Secondly, now that I'm back on my cancer medication and can stop being so neurotic about risking my health, I can also give my body a break whilst trying for the same outcome. A baby that is half of my husband, and can be cared for by me, its mother, from the moment it is born. This requires passing the medical toll on to someone else, but it would be someone willing, and having been through it myself, I'm confident it would be OK. I'm confident anyone who signs up for surrogacy, in properly regulated countries at least, knows the physical costs and are OK with them. For me, my body has been battered. Herein marks the end of a full decade of medical invasion. Cancer treatment, scans, surgery, chemotherapy, radiotherapy, more surgery, needles, giant needles every month for ten years, drugs, more drugs, more needles. Brief rest, and then fertility treatment, more scans, more needles, injecting myself with needles, ugh. It saw me change from a perfectly healthy needle-phobe, to a world-weary, decidedly less-healthy one with very many scars to prove it. Any kind of medical treatment is always going to be a trigger for me. It will be a relief to step away and give my body and my cortisol production a rest.

Thirdly, I can stop beating myself up emotionally as well as physically. Taking on a team member helps me put things into perspective. I can see it from Mr B's point of view now. If our surrogate had a failed transfer cycle, I would never blame her, so why did I blame myself? Being on the outside does wonders for rationalising things. I can stop feeling so guilty every time my own damn body fails, and be in a better position to understand how someone else might feel going through a similar thing. But with a better chance of success!

Having a baby at newborn stage would give me something close to the full experience I didn't think I'd be able to achieve. I know it isn't necessary for loving or bonding, I know so many women don't get that opportunity, but there is a chance I can, so of course I want to take it.

And then there are the cons.

As I mentioned already, first and foremost is the issue of, well, I want to neatly summarise it as 'supply and demand', but that is highly inappropriate when we're talking about borrowing someone else's bodily function, so I absolutely will not. It's exactly the kind of language that exacerbates the anti-surrogacy activists, and yes it makes it all sound very transactional, but in a purely pragmatic way, it kind of is. (Only in some countries though, where money is involved and contracts are drawn up; England is not one of them.) The problem here is that way too many desperate people want and need a surrogate, and way too few pure-hearted people have it in them to volunteer to become one. Let me be very clear here: it is no small ask. So if you can stomach the thought of attending one of those 'surrogacy socials', you'd be vying for the attention of one altruistic angel to every thirty to sixty other couples. The thought of persuading someone to choose me over someone else in that context makes me wrinkle my nose involuntarily. It casts a bit of an ugly shadow on the whole thing. Not only would I have to be on my best behaviour, it would be better-than-YOU behaviour. And an 'every man for himself' compulsion among a room full of sad infertile couples doesn't sound like a party to me. Unless they have tequila.

Then there's that, the exploitation issue. Just writing the word fills me with abhorrence because I don't want to give any credence to the argument. Anyone, *anyone* who is sensible and wise would understand that yes, there is absolutely opportunity for exploitation where surrogacy is concerned, but surrogacy itself is not exploitative as a rule. When I was first researching the idea (research is vital by the way, especially for you misinformed anti-surrogacy keyboard warriors), I came across some worryingly high-ranking pieces of tosh that really shouldn't be allowed. For one, the journalism was terrible: 'Surrogacy may have been surrounded by an aura of Elton John-ish happiness, cute newborns and notions of the modern family, but behind that is an industry that buys and sells human life.' It's pretty inflammatory, it's not based in fact, but points for mentioning Elton because, I'm not sure if I mentioned, I do love him.

For another, I'm quite sure it's way off the mark. Here's another example: 'There has been a total commodification of human life: click: choose race and eye colour: pay; then have your child delivered.'

Now I'm no expert yet, but I'm under the impression that what I'm about to embark upon is more like fifteen months' worth of careful and considered devotion to the project of our lives, rather than a simple 'add to basket' scenario. Idiots.

What I will say is that where payment is possible, and agents can negotiate relationships between commissioning parents and surrogates, there is opportunity for transgression. Socially or financially vulnerable women might be lured by the money, without considering any emotional or physical impact, particularly in countries where the compensation fee might be ten times an average annual salary. There is a huge grey area across the surrogacy map of the world, and it is vitally important to me that I navigate it properly and carefully. So yes, this wider notion of 'surrogacy equals exploitation' is no doubt something we will come up against on a fairly regular basis, and that's an added worry for me. But it is also something I am here to undo. Misinformation and injustice really push my buttons.

Another con – feelings. I am a typical Scorpio, ergo I am prone to jealousy. Can I even cope with the idea of another woman sort of having a baby with my husband? How would I feel when the sonographer scans *her* stomach and not mine. Or when the baby kicks *her* ribs instead of squashing *my* bladder? The answer is I really don't know. I feel like I've come on exponentially in my acceptance of this crazy situation. There have been so many losses, and every single one means the goalposts move and I'm just desperately hoping to score at the next option. Right now the thought of another woman carrying my baby is absolutely amazing. Surreal, but amazing in the very fact that it's even an option for Mr B and me. If I can't do it myself, and I can't give up, then this is what comes next. Within that frame I feel like I'm going to be OK with it all, but really, who knows until it's happening to me, right?

Mr B, are you worried I'll be jealous? 'Fuck yes! That's just one out of a shitload of things I'm worried about. I don't want you to be sad about any of this, that's the thing.' He swears more when he's worried.

The legal issue is probably the biggest. In that it isn't legal. Well, it is and it isn't. It's complicated.

The UK upholds some, let's say 'archaic', laws regarding surrogacy. We have not been able to fundamentally change things since IVF first happened, and the Surrogacy Arrangements Act 1985 came to be. As an 'ill-considered and largely irrelevant panic measure' if you ask UCL professor Michael Freeman, it was rushed through parliament as an addendum, basically in response to the first British surrogacy case of 'Baby Cotton'. Rather than setting a framework for surrogacy going forward, the act was more of a fire-fighting afterthought, a knee-jerk response to press and public outcry when Kim Cotton gave birth to a baby for an anonymous European couple in exchange for £6500. 'Baby trafficking!' the headlines screamed. 'Quick! Establish a surrogacy postscript!' the government responded.

The main outcome was that surrogacy arrangements were to be legally unenforceable, with a parental order (transferring legal parentage from the surrogate) only to be granted retrospectively, some time after the birth. And no compensation could be paid whatsoever, making the practice only altruistic. Apparently, it was hoped that such restrictive measures would kind of extinguish the practice of surrogacy before it really took off.

So let me tell you what that looks like for me, from the mouth of Mr Hiyer, and why my jaw dropped to the floor while Mr B fell off his chair.

Firstly, the parental order wheels cannot be put in motion until six weeks after birth. For the first six weeks, the surrogate could change her mind if she wanted to. Keep the baby, see ya. And as my dad keeps calling me to worry about, 'She will have raging hormones, darling. I'm worried about a surrogate woman being irrational because of her hormones.' Even though I admonish him for being generalistic, in this context he has a very good point.

Secondly, and this bit is the ridiculous kicker, the birth certificate will state the surrogate as 'Mother'. It's just a birth certificate, and it can be amended after the parental order – provided she hasn't changed her mind and that part still happens, so I kind of get that. But it would also be the case if the eggs used were mine. Genetically I'd be the parent, but legally I wouldn't be. But that's moot here, it's not my egg. It *is* Mr B's sperm though, so is he on the birth certificate? Is he fuck. The role of 'Father' goes to the surrogate's husband. What's he done in this equation? Brought her cups of tea? Massaged her swollen ankles? The only way Mr B would get a legal look-in would be if the surrogate weren't married. Then he's drafted in as back-up Father. I could take a DNA test to the High Court to prove paternal parentage and they would still rule against him. See? ARCHAIC.

With these dumbfoundings, on top of the lack of any kind of regulation or contractual commitment, it all feels a bit slippery on my home soil.

There has been reform since the early Eighties, and things have improved slightly (I'd at least be eligible for maternity leave now, something that was previously available to the surrogate but not the mother. Who did they postulate would look after the baby while its parent was stuck at work? The cat?). But even with some reform, it's still precarious to say the least.

The long and short of it is, in terms of protection for both parties, you can draw up an altruistic surrogacy agreement, but it wouldn't be enforceable in a court of law. And yes, it's extremely rare that surrogacy cases even break down enough to get to court, and with an agreement in place chances are the court would agree in favour of the intended parents for custody, but still. That involves court! A court hearing. And angst and anguish and heartache whichever way the outcome goes.

This initial somewhat surprising discussion, and then later, my own research – fortifying glass of wine in hand – is not quite going the way I'd imagined. Frankly, it's a huge disappointment. I felt like surrogacy was a sigh of relief. Now, after this overload of information, it feels like a mountain I don't think I have the energy to climb. Mr B and I can barely bring ourselves to talk about it because the whole thing feels so overwhelming and unfair. How can it be that this country that I have loved and lived in my whole life, is so, well, obviously stupid. The fact is, society has changed, and it keeps changing. Alternative routes to parenthood have been perfectly normalised, but the laws haven't managed to keep up.

I hate that Mr B wouldn't be recognised as the father, even though he'd comprise half of the kid. I hate that an altruistic surrogacy 'contract' is essentially an informal agreement based on trust.

I am a control freak with no control over my baby-making abilities. Imagine having to implicitly trust a stranger to carry and deliver a baby with the knowledge that they could change their mind up to six weeks after the birth because of the total lack of regulation.

In my own country that is. America, on the other hand …

6.

How does surrogacy work in America, exactly?

It's complicated. In a good and a bad way. At this point, I think it's more good than bad, but we'll see.

First things first, Mr B and I went back, very heavy-hearted, and talked to Mr Hiyer about our alternative options. Technically I'm not really a patient of his anymore, since my body is off the table – literally and metaphorically – but I feel like he's the right person to tell me what to do. I need affirmative action, otherwise I'll spiral into a pit of disappointment and regret. This is the first time in my life I've been pissed off with my own place of birth. Shame on you Britain, with your stupid approach to surrogate baby birth certificates and your slapdash, panic-driven law-addenda.

Our main stumbling block is this – we can't do the UK. We don't know anyone here who would be willing to act as our surrogate. We can't abide the thought of selling ourselves at a surrogacy social, and we feel quite a strong need to escape the incongruous and antiquated surrogacy laws.

We also – very important this bit – need to make sure we're avoiding the same kind of objectionable attitude we experienced in loosely regulated Russia. Therefore – sorry to you countries who've done nothing more than neighbour the place that fills us with trepidation – East is out. It's not you, it's us. We need rules and conformity. This is the biggest commitment of our lives, it's our future child we're talking about. We need to regain some semblance of control now.

For very many reasons, Mr Hiyer tells us, the USA is considered the gold standard in surrogacy practice. Mostly because it is so highly regulated, and it has to be that way because, to put it bluntly, it's a huge commercial business worth around $2.5billion at last count. Woah.

And so this multi-billion dollar industry, like all commercial businesses, is governed by legal precedent. In America surrogacy is legal under state law, meaning each state has its own rules around recognising legal parentage to a child born through surrogacy, and it's still fully illegal in some, including Nebraska and Michigan. New York only came off that list when it passed a surrogates' bill of rights in April 2020. So we won't be going to Nebraska or Michigan. But wherever we do end up will have rules and regulations and accountability and contracts. Ahh, sweet, sweet regulations.

So about that; the 'industry' thing. This is where the UK and the USA differ in their extremes. Whereas the UK only legalises altruistic surrogacy, in the USA it's referred to as commercial surrogacy. Whilst I hate that it's called that – it feels so impersonal, so transactional – it addresses the HUGE gaping hole that the British Surrogacy Act left wide open enough to scare us away. In that standardising and recognising the practice offers the control, the comfort, the regulation, the legality and the standard of service we are pinning our hopes on. I sometimes wonder if we'd feel so strongly about that criteria had Russia not been such a shit show. I suspect we'd probably have sucked it up and gone to a surrogacy social event on our own soil, plastered on a smile and done some discordant schmoozing. We'd have lived with the antiquated birth certificate – it's just a piece of paper after all – we'd have checked our emotions into rehab and got on with it, like we've done at every hurdle thus far. But ultimately, I just want to rest for once. I want to let my shoulders refrain from touching my earlobes. There's nothing wrong with that, right?

Well, wait, let's not get carried away here. There is that all important *commercial* part of commercial surrogacy to contend with first. The astronomical cost. There's quite a lot wrong with that for us, two hard-workers with a mortgage and zero savings. Mr Hiyer casually lets us know it's likely to be something to the tune of seventy-five to a hundred K.

Hold.

The.

Phone. 'WHY?' I whine, inside.

No really though, why?

Because of all the regulation I'm so keen to establish I guess. First of all, the legal fees. We'd need a UK lawyer *and* a US attorney. Same thing, but it's more fun using the appropriate language. We'll need to pay an agency a retainer fee to find us a surrogate and then manage the relationship to all intents and purposes. We'll need to pay frankly extortionate private US medical fees, and then we'd pay the surrogate a fee (the crucial difference) of something around $40,000, also known as 'compensation'. Which strikes me as quite sad sounding, when you put it in the context of the British altruistic model versus this here commercial one. The term 'altruistic' suggests that the surrogate takes some pleasure in offering this amazing gift. Compensation sounds like the opposite. Hmm. And fuck, that is a fucking hell of a lot of fucking money for fuck's sake, for anybody. Even Elton Joh— no, actually he's probably OK with it.

The thing is, it doesn't particularly feel like we have an option. Yes, we could go back to Russia, or Greece or Ukraine or anywhere else the internet offers as an amazing and 'affordable' place to do surrogacy. But after the experience we've just had, and the money we've already wasted, it feels irresponsible to risk losing even more. What if we choose the less expensive route, just like we did with Russia, and we plough more and more money in, only for it to fail or fall down like the last time. No. I need some kind of guarantee – wherever that might be possible in this very strange situation we've stumbled our way into. And yes, America seems to be the place to really offer it. This is really quite simple for me; I can only compare the feeling to being in debt to some kind of mafia. It is a decidedly undesirable, somewhat terrifying situation I'm in, but the alternative is inconceivable, threatening even, and so I have no choice but to find the money. So, carry on. Tell me more.

That's about all Mr Hiyer could tell us though, the rest was down to due diligence, research and then a bit more research. This overcoming-infertility project is becoming a full-time profession. Whilst Mr B sets about looking into 'Best Surrogacy Agencies USA', I do the only thing I can think of and try to get some trusted recommendations from someone who's been through it. Try finding one of those, though. Anyone? Anyone I know been through commercial surrogacy in the States and can give me some guidance? No one, really? Sadly, and inconceivably, I'm still not friends with Elton John, so it seems I'm left with good old, sometimes trustworthy Google. Google tells me a famous fashion designer who I'm sure vaguely knows a friend of a friend actually did do that exact thing, so with my mafia-debt determination I swallow any vestige of pride and try as many lines of communication as I can. Until, by some miracle, I have a phone call date set in place with the fashion designer's husband. Wow. I already feel part of some kind of underdog community; we're all equals here. We've got each other's backs

I am away in the country for the weekend and go outside for some privacy. The conversation – which takes place standing very still in the one precarious spot of signal in the middle of nowhere – is enlightening, purely because

I've never spoken to anyone who's done surrogacy before. It already feels quite exotic even before I think about who it is giving me the advice. The husband of a fashion designer, whose show I've sat at in every fashion week for most of my career, and whose garments I've lusted after for just as long. In fact, I wore a jacket of his to keep me warm on my wedding day, and here I am pouring my heart out to his other half and hearing their backstory in return. Granted, it is a bit different for a very well-off gay couple who always planned on having their family this way, rather than a heterosexual couple who were somewhat derailed somewhere along the line. For one, there are a ton of specialist agencies geared towards making surrogacy for gay parents and the LGBTQ+ community possible. Unsurprisingly, in the commercial context, with surrogacy being one of only two routes to parenthood for gay males, it means they're likely the demographic that boosts most of the billions. Surrogacy is also totally off the table to them in many other countries (and even a couple of US states) that only allow heterosexual couples or single females to commission a surrogate. Outrageous, I know.

He tells me he got a list of the top ten agencies for gay dads from his friend who also did surrogacy in the States, so he promises to share it with me, assuming the service they offer is all much of a muchness. He also tells me he did three trips over to have face-to-face meetings and really ascertain which agency was best for him. 'It's important to get a good feeling about the people who are going to be facilitating this very special process,' he says. I wholeheartedly agree, all the while certain that I will not be making any face-to-face decision-making trips whilst we're still trying to work out how we'll afford this gold-standard process.

I finish the call feeling glowy from finally speaking to someone who represents the happy result of what we're trying to embark upon. And also, I'm now armed with The List, which at least helps me cut through the deluge of overwhelming internet marketing. Like this: 99.3 per cent success rates! The fastest route to parenthood on the West Coast! Turn your dream into a reality, guaranteed! Which damn one to click?

So here we are. This right here is where our surrogacy journey starts. Mr B and I spend yet another evening at our laptops, this time shopping for a surrogacy agent. One who will apparently find us our surrogate, an egg donor, a counsellor, a fertility doctor and embryologist, an escrow accountant (a what?), and also hook us up with an attorney. It strikes me again that traditionally one shouldn't need to enlist this many outsiders in the act of baby making (unless, of course, that kind of thing floats your boat). I'll tell you what floats Mr B's boat: diligent, thorough research. He is very much into it. Even though I'm not finding it the sexiest way to spend an evening, slumping – OK, sulking – on the sofa, he is at his organisational best, pinging emails and arranging initial consultations. It's frankly heroic. Maybe it does feel kind of romantic after all.

The best advice I got from my fashion designer phone call was to go with an agency we have a good feeling about; we need to make some sort of connection. How you do that across an ocean is the question, but this is such a personal experience we need delicate handlers, I guess. And so, to start with, we work our way through his list.

The cost is the part that is really difficult to ascertain, because it seems to differ wildly depending on where we look. Research (thank you, Mr B) tells us we can expect to pay around £20k for medical expenses, £50k for surrogate compensation, and other expenses, the agency and legal fees et cetera, around another £15k. So according to the internet, it'll be about £85,000. Ho.ly.shit.

That's compared to around £30,000 in the Ukraine or Georgia, £65,000 in Greece and, well, nothing here in England, except for 'reasonable expenses'. I think the fact that we already have an appointment booked with a financial advisor for a couple of days' time is testament to a) how much we were burnt by our Russian experience, b) how desperate we are to be parents and c) how fortuitous it was that we bought our (only now) lovely house in the (only now) nice area at the time that we did. We think we can find the money, we just need to make sure we do it right this time. After all, we will never regret spending our money on our child. That's what parents do, right? We're just starting way earlier and, well, maybe gambling a little with the poor kid's university fees but, who knows, without my genes they might not be inclined to go to university anyway. Only kidding Mr B, you also have the genetic means to make this child a genius, I know, I know.

The first agency we tried didn't get back to us for a full week, so we scratched them off the list. Could be a sign that they don't care enough about new clients, could be an admin error, either way, I'm out.

The next one sent a perfunctory response, attaching their fees list with all the possible options laid out, as if we had asked how much for a cut and colour with a senior stylist please. No personal touch, next!

The third sent a much nicer response of a similarly generic nature.

> We understand choosing an agency is an extremely important decision, and we are honored to possibly have the opportunity to assist you in your family building journey.

Promising! And then, when I mailed back to enquire about setting up a Skype chat at very short notice, she said:

> Oh absolutely! When is best for you? I can make some time later this afternoon if you like.

Yes, we like. Is this the considerate nature and personal feeling Fashion Husband was telling me about? It feels VERY exciting, and really quite special. Extra special if you think about it. I think I'm drunk on adrenalin, which is not the best way to make 'extremely important decisions', but we arrange to Skype with Lacey, the Genesis Consultancy patient coordinator, later that same afternoon. I get busy scribbling down my questions, as if I'm interviewing to fill a role on my team, but in the end it didn't matter because the other two agencies we also managed to speak to were outdone within about thirty seconds. They didn't hold a candle to Lacey and her soft, friendly approach. But at least they managed to get back to us at all I suppose, because none of the others we reached out to did. Gosh, surrogacy business in the States must be booming. Genesis Consultants promise to act as a liaison service for the Intended Parents (us) and the Surrogate (who? Who knows?!). This comprises setting us up with all the aforementioned necessary team members, sorting the logistics, but also, Lacey emphasises, they will encourage communication throughout the whole process to ensure a positive and healthy relationship between all parties involved. That's the part I feel the most nervous about. They'll be like a chaperone. This, on top of all the red tape stuff, means we can finally take a breather, right? This feels … right.

Next, Lacey gently takes us through the approximate process and then an indigestion-inducing fee breakdown, and I manage to only cry three times during the entire conversation. I don't know why I get so annoyingly emotional when it comes to this; I'm taking medication that suppresses my hormones for goodness' sake.

And so we make the decision. Like my method for choosing wine on the wine list, Genesis Consultants are not the cheapest, but nowhere near the most expensive. That makes them just right in my book. Lacey, and then their CEO Zoe, both tell us that at a worst-case scenario we shouldn't ever need to spend more than $90,000. 'What comprises worst-case scenario?' I ask nervously. 'Well, if it doesn't work the first time and you need to do another round of IVF say, that kind of thing.' Well, that doesn't sound too bad. I had five failed rounds myself, surely bad luck can't keep striking the same tree, *surely*.

When you start talking in the new realms of that much bloody money, it almost becomes abstract. It's like Monopoly money. The same thing happened when I planned our wedding: Oh, you only charge £90 to light two tiki torches? That's amazing! Mr B, I managed to get the tiki torch lighting for just £70 (always knock some off when retelling any cost-story). He still doesn't know what I spent on the flowers. But I digress. This is all starting to feel weirdly doable.

If our financial advisor agrees to us borrowing against the house, then we are going to have a blinking BABY! By when? This time next year? When? WHEN?

When we finish our call, Lacey emails over the timeline and *rapidly deflates* oh God, it feels so bloody long.

First, we pay them a retainer fee, then they go about matching us with a surrogate. Apparently this can take anywhere between three and five months. Well that already feels insurmountable. If I round it up and exaggerate a tiny bit, that's half a year gone on nothing. Then, by month seven or eight, the surrogate will hopefully get 'medical clearance', but only hopefully. If she doesn't we have to start the matching process again. But assuming she does, then we can proceed to the legal bit. Legal clearance happens at around month nine, which is also when the egg donation and embryo creation part starts. Again? It feels like we did that only yesterday, and it took such a long time then too.

Then the usual, the part we've done before, but this time someone else steps into my role. Preparation for embryo transfer, embryo transfer, Two Week Wait – very remotely this time. Transatlantically in fact – and then pregnancy and then, boom, around eighteen months later, BABY! It does sort of feel like a bit of a prison sentence, after a good year and a half of trying already, to know that there's no chance of motherhood anytime in my immediate future. But it's very positive action. Expensive, positive action. Expensive, positive, professionally regulated action that means I can finally take my foot off the pedal, put my trust in a whole team on the other side of the pond, and look forward to doing this thing right this time.

Our sweet FA said yes, by the way, so this is it. We are doing this! With an audible gulp we pressed PAY and ping across the agency registration fee, we remark at how inappropriate and strange it is to receive a baby-making receipt in return, and then we go to bed as if our lives haven't just taken an entirely unchartered new direction. I sleep surprisingly well, too.

7.

Why don't you just adopt?

Ah, good question. I'm messing with you, it's a terrible question. And trust me, one you shouldn't ask someone who is going through any kind of infertility saga, because it will never be a) something they haven't thought of themselves yet or b) any of your business. I will say it's a valid question, but it depends on whether you say it out loud or not. If I may, I'd like to pick this apart a little, so maybe you don't have to say it out loud (don't say it out loud), but you can still get an answer.

So, are you ready? Then we'll begin. The question of adoption is a delicate and complex topic. It is sensitive by its very necessity, but put very simply, adoption is absolutely not the responsibility of the infertile, and I straight up refuse to allow such a reductive treatment of such an amazing and difficult thing.

I can't and haven't ruled it out, by the way. That's not why I'm so vehemently preoccupied with explaining why I didn't 'just adopt'. No, it's because it still remains the most asked question of all time (in my universe only, not in the world, ever).

'Why don't you just adopt?'

And I get it; we are taking a huge and expensive leap into a still questionable practice (in that there are questions, ones I still have, as well as the moral and ethical ones that other people might toss around their own minds). We are embarking upon months and months of appointments and contracts and money and lawyers and doctors and hopes that we're about to invest fully, without a guaranteed positive outcome. All of this might justify the question like never before. But I still want to talk about it here, because it deserves its own explanation, rather than a mere sideline scenario, or unsung rebuttal.

First off, the semantics. Because this simple question has shifting connotations, and they all hinge on the word 'just'.

'Just' implies adoption is the easier alternative to surrogacy. In our instance it is true that it would be less expensive, but that's about where the 'easier' bit ends. 'Just' undermines the amazing importance and effort and hard work that goes into adopting. I am just as much in awe of parents who can adopt as I am of women who can act as surrogates. I'm also lucky enough to know a few such parents, so I often talk to them about it to try to fully understand. Understanding also means I can both appreciate their superheroism, and also allows me to make an informed decision about what path we're going to go down now. Ergo, this is a conscious decision Mr B and I have made, having carefully considered all of our options.

Like I said before, it's totally fine to wonder about the alternative options, of course it is, but it *should* be obvious that we have thought about it, too.

If you're interested in making your understandable curiosity more valid, take the 'just' out of the sentence. The 'Why don't you adopt?' question *is* pertinent. There you go! In fact, I'd say at this point I get asked it at least once a week on average, like this recent example: 'With world population approaching nine billion would it not be better to save the heartache and adopt an unwanted child?' That was dropped into my DMs by a Mr Smith.

Thank you Mr Smith, I do see your point. We are an infertile couple struggling to have a baby, and there are millions of children in need of a loving home. I get it and I feel it and my heart also hurts for those children who, yes, I could potentially offer a home to. But, um, so could you. So could my friend Carla, who is due to give birth to her fourth child any day now. So could my nine or ten friends who are dabbling in the early stages of IVF right now, or my other friend Nat, who had her two kids early, so is ready for another go round the merry-go-round at the age of thirty-five maybe? I doubt Mr Smith would suggest they should have adopted had he seen their bumps, or grown-up kids, or busy treatment protocol schedules in the queue at Sainsbury's. Obviously adopting children is not an exercise in population control. I'm being facetious by suggesting that's what Mr Smith meant there, but I also believe wholeheartedly that it is not the responsibility of us people who struggle to conceive to adopt children.

In my mind adoption is as incomparable to surrogacy as a natural pregnancy is – a different route to parenthood open to fertile *and* infertile people, and as such we'll cross that bridge when and if we come to it. Maybe for number two, who knows?

Even in the far distance, though, it feels somewhat overwhelming. Precisely because it is not a small thing to take on a child in need. It's an admirable thing, a wonderfully fulfilling thing, but it is not a fall-back safety net for when fertility goes wrong. It's not even a good deed. It's a HUGE deed, and it takes very strong people and a long and tough process. For instance, there are thorough and intrusive assessment stages, home visits, no stones left unturned, no medical record or bank account unscrutinised, zero skeletons in any closets. There is even a panel assessment that most people I've spoken to about this liken to the biggest job interview of their lives. One that you can prepare for, but you'll never know how. This is just the build-up, the preparation. All of which I could do, I know I could if I had to, but the reality of what happens next is the profound part I don't think I'm ready to adjust to yet.

In our country, most children are placed for adoption after being removed from a situation that is no longer safe. While there are relatively rare situations where parents can decide to have their baby adopted pre-birth – known as 'relinquished babies' – the most common age bracket of children needing homes is two to five. What this statement amounts to is as much an intimidating reality for me and Mr B as it would be for you, or for my friend Carla, or Nat, or even for Mr Smith.

I would suddenly have a child in my home with some fundamental and specific needs on top of the ordinary parenting that I'm already daunted by. If I'm perfectly honest, it feels like an overwhelming responsibility. I'm not by any means saying I could not, or would not, step up to the plate, I'm saying it's not as simple as falling in love with a whole new person and living happily ever after. And I truly believe that this admirable job should not be a plaster to stick over the failures of the infertile. In fact, most adoption agencies would require extra assessments and *more* time to ensure we'd emotionally come to terms with not having our own baby, come to terms with everything thereafter and finally come to terms with the end of this whole process. We'd be broken people looking to adopt a broken child from a broken home and that, obviously, is not an ideal equation, for anybody concerned.

I wouldn't be brave enough to commit my presupposing to paper, had I not had it reinforced by experienced friends, but more so by experienced professionals who've messaged me when I've spoken about it before:

'I have worked with a lot of adopted children over the years and each one is unique and special. To be in a position where they are put up for adoption, they will have been through hell and suffered horrendous conditions. In fact, it's actually quite rare for this decision to be made. Usually authorities will try to support family structures, or place children with biological family first. Basically, to be put up for adoption means all other options have been exhausted. These children deserve to be someone's *first* choice, not their last resort.'

And thankfully, there are people who willingly reverse my route to parenthood. They'd only resort to surrogacy, or even later a natural pregnancy, if adoption wasn't possible for them. Those people are an extra-special breed, and exactly the kinds of parents children in need, well, need. The expert continues:

'I find it frustrating that people assume once the child is placed in a loving home all will be well. This is simply not true. The children often have severe trauma and attachment disorders. To successfully support adoptive children, specialist care and nurture is needed. Therapeutic parenting is very demanding and often totally misunderstood by people outside of the adoption circle. Adoption is a wonderful experience but it's not easy. It's also not for everyone.'

My friends Adam and Kenny spent about a year going through the process and adopted a little boy over the age of five, since this is sadly the demographic that is least successfully rehomed. In ugly terms, 'the least popular demographic'. You see? Very special breed.

Adam told me it was supremely tough for the first year, and one of the hardest bits was the expectation. 'No one tells you it's OK to feel bad sometimes. Tired, a bit depressed or traumatised even. I now know it's like any new parent feels, but we didn't feel we could complain about it because we'd adopted. That kind of pressure makes you feel like you're failing, when actually it's totally normal.'

As he's explaining this to me, I feel seen. Yes, that will be me! I know I will feel that with the surrogate baby I've already tried so hard for, before we've even got going. If all goes well, I will witness a pregnancy from afar, and then I'll be handed a brand new person without knowing him or her from the inside. Except my sudden new family member wouldn't have come to me with a history that I might not be equipped to save them from. So there's no 'just' in it. Adoption is profoundly courageous, and everyone who does it, including Adam and Kenny, are heroes in my eyes.

I know adoption is also a wonderful opportunity – for both the children who can have their lives transformed and for the adoptive parents, whether they're fertile, infertile, single, same-sex, in a threesome (is that allowed? One bonus extra parent?). But for my husband and I? First, we have the opportunity to try to have a baby who is genetically related to Mr B. He, at least, has the chance to have his own child, and it's a choice and a right that we welcome. That we're undeniably grateful for, in fact.

I suspect, with this question, there are broader social expectations at play here. As humans, we are conditioned and expected to want a baby more than anything. Well this is me, trying. The biology and psychology behind surrogacy is fascinating and painful all at the same time. And everyone has their own limitations attached. I wonder why I didn't stop after three failed rounds of IVF. I wonder why one failed pregnancy didn't tip me over the edge, why I went on to have another one. Surrogacy is epic, in an entirely different way to adoption. But it's not too much, or too far, for us at least. How much is too much to want a baby anyway? And why do we need to justify it at all? If you want to keep your friends' appreciation of you at the highest level, take the 'just' out when you ask them the question. Or don't ask it at all.

If anyone finds themselves confronted with the A-word query, let me help you out with a very poignant and concise response:

'Why don't YOU just adopt (bozo)?' That part in parentheses can be muttered into whatever it is you're drinking.

I genuinely hope I'd be able to embrace adoption with my whole heart one day, maybe for a future child, who knows? But right now half of my heart is consumed with fertilising in a petri dish somewhere, someday, waiting for the chance to complete this particular story. I'm going to concentrate on that hope as long as it feels right for Mr B and me, no regrets or what-ifs.

8.

How do you even find a surrogate?

Sometimes I look in the mirror and think 'woah'. This is me. Normal, ordinary, had-a-lovely-life-thus-far me (we'll gloss over the cancer part), and I'm about to try to have a baby via surrogacy. It's mental! And, hang on, it's grossly overwhelming and so stratospherically out of my comfort zone and I have no idea how I'm supposed to get my head around growing a baby in another woman's womb. And then my heart races a bit and I start to get that inward whooshing, trippy feeling, like I need to steady the room by putting my hands on the wall, so you know what I do? I stop looking in the mirror. I blink, put the TV on – ah yes, TV, so normal and banal and mind-numbing that I don't need to think too much about my reality. The problem with that coping mechanism is it's not very productive. It's not conducive to getting this crazy show on the road. I still find it best to disassociate myself from this breathtaking rollercoaster as much as possible, whilst cracking on with organising and facilitating it. It's the only way to cope. I am 'journalist-me'. Embarking on a highly fascinating and unusual storyline that I was not expecting. It's just that it's happening to emotional me rather than some other subject I'd normally be reading or writing about. So I park emotional me as much as possible (she tends to emerge at 3 a.m. or in the middle of important meetings to have a little cry and/or panic attack, but that's to be expected), and instead focus on getting shit done.

So, now we're officially signed with Genesis Consultants, but where and when does one actually *begin*? This agency will be our administrative middle man, there to take out all of the legwork. They have carefully enlisted and screened surrogates on their books whom they match to their 'Intended Parent' clients, or IPs, and so, first and foremost, we need to deal with the biggest beast – this matching process. We've been assigned our own surrogacy coordinator called Jane, who seems nice enough – as nice as you can find someone you haven't had a chance to meet in real life, who is tasked with changing your life forever. She reminds us that finding a suitable surrogate takes somewhere between three to five months. That's because, whilst there are surrogates already on the books, this agency has around sixty intended parent couples to every agent, like Jane. If that seems like way too many, that's because it is, but we had no clue at this point. Then we have the legal bit, the medical checks, not to mention the egg donation process. Very best case we're looking at is around fifteen months, maybe a year and a half, before I can realistically become a mum. For the clinically infertile, the previous triers and failures, this is practically a lifetime. Another Christmas or two to watch go past, countless weeks and months of work. A couple of years older, depending on where your birthday falls. Gah! But good also, because we have no other choice here and this is definitive progress. Get us on that wait list Jane, and do it pronto.

The matching process is something like MySingleFriend on MDMA. It's definitely weird. And extra. Since there are sixty other couples vying for Jane's attention, and a perfect match just like us, the surrogate gets to choose her IPs. To do that she needs something to go on, so we fill out a profile to promote ourselves as the most wholesome, loving, deserving parents to be possible. There will always be criteria we cannot possibly fulfil. For example, Jane tells us a lot of her surrogates have specified that they only want to help American citizens, say. Or similarly, religious people, or gay couples or white couples, the list goes on. Mr B and I are a straight, mixed-race couple of agnostic foreigners. That we cannot control, but our personal statements we can knock out the park. We write each other's one evening – as per agency directive – and I feel a bit like I'm auditioning my husband for someone else to love. I outline his most wonderful characteristics, his supremely fantastic nature, the reasons I fell in love with him that would also make him the most supreme father in existence. I make out he has no discernable faults, one hundred per cent person-perfection, and he does the same for me. It's kind of funny and uncomfortable at the same time. Why do we need to sell ourselves so magnanimously for the chance at becoming a parent? Who is this anonymous collection of American strangers that gets to decide who is more deserving of the opportunity based on their religious beliefs or aggrandised characteristics? There are people as evil as Fred and Rosemary West who didn't have to audition for the privilege of becoming parents, but we do, simply because we couldn't do it naturally?! Injustice winds me right up, by the way. We finish our forms and let our hearts swell at each other's loving characterisation, and then we send them off to Jane and wait for the next stage.

Meanwhile, we collectively work on the other matching process, the egg donor. The American agency has their own in-house donor programme. That means they actively recruit, pre-screen and background check each potential egg donor before they can join The Agency database, where people like me then stipulate our requirements (for us at this point, it is literally 'vague similarity wherever it matters') and we find a match. The supremely crucial part that effectively replaces my initial faulty contribution. We are matched with donor no. 234, who will provide the 'me' part of the embryo equation. She is white, with dark hair, dark eyes and cute baby pictures that you could say bear a passing resemblance to me if you squint hard enough. You're only allowed to see baby pictures, although some US databases show the donors as teenagers or even present-day pictures too. I think I would find that too much of a lasting visual impression, a bit of an emotional conflict, so I'm happy to just trust in these experts and start the exciting process that will one day result in our CHILD. SO obscure.

By this point we don't care in the slightest how close the match is, we are just grateful to get what we're given. I guess we'll find out what that looks like in fifteen months or so, right? Best-case scenario willing.

And best-fertility doctor willing, also. Because that bit is crucial to this all going our way, and it's another part of this hugely scary process that is handled by Genesis. They promise to connect us with the finest fertility specialist in the closest proximity to our donor. That's how it works over there, because she will need to go back and forth to his clinic much more often than our eventual surrogate will, so it makes sense to pick someone in the same state. They tell us about Dr Hernandez.

Dr Hernandez is apparently something of a big deal round these parts – these parts being Miami, where both he and donor no. 234 are based. Jane at Genesis tells us he's simply wonderful, they've worked with him loads before, his manner is great, his success rates even better, they cannot recommend him highly enough. Which is lucky because we have zero clue how we'd even begin to find someone reputable enough to take on this very important role in our lives without them. So, excitingly, we now have a donor and a doctor!

And while we let that information and double act settle into place and take up their natural order in the process at some point soon, we wait – again – for the biggest piece of the puzzle to land in our inbox.

The first surrogacy match.

We receive the email earlier than expected. Three days after we signed on the proverbial line. I'm sitting in the pub after work with my colleagues, quietly and privately processing the surrogacy timeline, trying not to get disheartened at the sentence I can see stretched out before me. It's a funny one to talk about with other people – a bit like my experience of cancer. It's super exotic and morbidly fascinating, but also nothing anyone around this table can relate to, so the conversation becomes a bit awkward. Irritating even. It's easier to give topline and then wait for it to be brought up again, which, depending on the crowd, might never happen. This group is talking about something I am not concentrating on whatsoever, but I nod and smile in all the right places, so I don't think they have any idea. Instead, I am going over the logistics in my addled head. Between three and nine months to even find a match is a long time. In three months I will have had another birthday, so technically will be a whole year older. It'll be approaching Christmas – will it be the best yet or another worst? Well and truly out of the table conversation now, I pick up my phone and absent-mindedly check Instagram, Twitter, emails in that order. DING, one comes through from The Agency while I'm looking at the screen.

'Profile, Surrogate Louise' says the subject.

'BADOOMBADOOM' says my suddenly racing heart, out loud, I'm quite sure of it. A quick scan and blah blah, 'the reason for me contacting you ...' blah, 'some wonderful news ...' yes yes? 'has reviewed your profile and she is very interested in proceeding to the next step if you feel mutually.'

Grammatically odd and abrupt end to the sentence, but we'll gloss over that because WE HAVE A MATCH! Already! Three short days into the three to nine months projected. Wowza. Louisa (profile attached) was a surrogate with The Agency last year, delivering a baby girl for a couple from France; and apparently she is looking forward to another journey.

Well hold the phone, please caller. Stop everything you're doing everyone round this table, I must message my husband immediately! We excitedly WhatsApp back and forth about how this is meant to be, and how we will obviously smash all the usual rules and fly through this surrogacy thing because we bloody deserve it by now. Obviously, three days for the match instead of the three months most people take means we've got this! We are highly matchable! It takes one swift and slightly inebriated skim of Louisa's profile to fall utterly in love with her. She's perfect, isn't she? Because she wants to do this for us. And she looks a bit like our friend Debbie. Yes! Yes YES! It's a yes from us. We *do* feel mutually.

A week later we received a perfunctory email from The Agency to say, in not so many words, 'Whoopsie! Our bad. Louisa is incompatible, actually. She's had six children, you see, and another pregnancy would put her health at too much risk to meet the doctor's criteria. So, um, yes we shouldn't have even shown her your profile, let alone got your hopes waaay up so soon. Back to the drawing board, yeah?'

The Agency's first fuck-up. Leading to my first – ha ha, who am I kidding – my one of many meltdowns. An introduction to the confounding complications of surrogacy in the USA. It all depends on the right agency you see. Trust me when I say, you need a good one.

Then, we fit the timeline a bit better, which at least is reassuring in some tiny way. Several months and a birthday later, we get a similar email, this time introducing us to Maxine. Maxine is a psychotherapist who wants to be a surrogate. Sounds amazing, right? Physicians in the States are paid exceptionally well, so we can safely assume she doesn't need the money. Her motivation must be altruistic. This could mean the best of both worlds: a British moral approach with an American regulated industry behind the whole process. Dr Hernandez is impressed. 'A physician!' he smiles at us over his desk, where we're sat, meeting him face to face for the first time. 'That is highly unusual. Lucky you! If all goes well with her medical checks we would probably manage an embryo transfer in a few months.'

We were of course in Miami when we had that conversation. A necessary trip so that Mr B can make his, ahem, *deposit*. It's a funny old game, eh? Nine hours each way so that my husband can essentially have the most expensive wank in the world.

Meeting Dr Hernandez was a much bigger deal than I expected it to be. His accent is almost as thick as his moustache, and he is ridiculously tall, six foot seven at least, which made him imposing even before he ushered us into his room to, essentially, grill us about who we were, why we needed him and how our ovaries might fare one day if left to their own devices. That last one was just directed at me, but it was a weird enough line of questioning under these circumstances that both Mr B and I were quite taken aback. I still don't know why he needed so much background on me specifically, since I wouldn't be the one who was remotely medically involved in the whole process. We were in his cluttered office for about ten minutes all in and, even though his manner was sort of odd, we came away feeling supremely reassured. He was confident to the point of seeming nonchalant, which apparently is enough to raise our hopes right through the roof so, Thank you Dr Hernandez, we look forward to working with you.

Afterwards, when he was finally allowed a well-earned beer on the beach, I mentioned what had been niggling me since we received the email from Zoe at The Agency. 'Isn't there something or other about therapists being the ones who need the most therapy?' I ventured. He'd never heard that adage, which was enough reassurance for me, so we boarded the plane home, happy and hopeful. Maxine sounded amazing, wonderful, perfect in fact. The funny thing about reading the profile of a woman who wants to lend her body to your most desperate cause is that you feel a strong attachment to her before you've even got to the last page. It's because she not only put herself up for this amazing thing – seemingly with the very best motivation in this case – but that she *chose* us, out of all the people she could have chosen.

Ahh, that lovely warm glow lasted all the way to Heathrow airport, when we turned off airplane mode and the emails came through. I paraphrase, but you'll get the gist: 'Hey! Hope you had a fun trip! Yeah, sorry guys, unfortunately Maxine isn't mentally well enough to be a surrogate. She has suffered from manic depression for several years now, which we probably should have flagged internally here before we got in touch with you again, since it's obvious that the psychological effect of giving up a baby might be a bit iffy in this case. But hey, we're only human! So, once again, back to the old drawing board, yeah?

CRUSHING DISAPPOINTMENT. We've had our hopes raised and slaughtered twice already and by now I'm losing faith in our choice of agency. Truth be told, I spend some nights sweating myself to sleep. We kind of, sort of, let our emotions carry us away and signed our future over to some people we just had a nice feeling about. I try not to dwell on what bad instinct I've had about other important people in my life who have ended up doing me right over in the end, and instead convince myself I'm entirely confident in a successful outcome. Look in the mirror and repeat after me, 'I AM NOT AN IDIOT. I AM ENTIRELY CONFIDENT IN A SUCCESSFUL OUTCOME.'

We found out later that had Maxine passed her psychological evaluation and we had proceeded, we would have been crippled by the costs, since her high physician's salary means her American insurance premiums are also humongous. Plus, we would have to cover her loss of earnings for any pre-, during and post-pregnancy downtime. They didn't think of that, either.

But we can trust in the donor egg train chugging its way to the station, right? Um. Not really, but the one thing we have is time, so let's not worry too much about prioritising our embryo-making in the meantime, OK? Especially if we aren't bothered about being the oldest people at the school gates or dying before we've met any grandchildren. Sure! For some strange reason, nothing has been happening on that side of things until we make all the enquiries and The Agency finally gets the ball rolling. Just like any surrogate on the books, the egg donors also have to go through a psychological, then medical screening. Also we need to do 'legal clearance', which means finding an attorney in their state, appointing our own attorney, a lot of back and forth between them both to finalise a contract, and then the whole egg extraction medical protocol starts. We find out that first we need to pay to send her for a basic fertility test. A what now? A basic fertility test. You know, to check if she has any, you know, fertility. Oh yes, yes, people can appear on The Agency egg donor database without knowing if they are able to donate any eggs.

Sigh.

If it sounds time consuming, that's because it really, really is. There is no reason The Agency couldn't have started this the moment we were matched with donor no. 234. I'm not sure exactly what we're paying this agency fee for at this point, but I'm loathe to question them in case they turn around and dump us unceremoniously, like Dr Solokov in St Petersburg. It seems agonisingly frustrating that we have to pay the highest premium for someone to ease our way through this alien territory, only for them to, well, not really be very capable thus far. And then fear complaining because they literally have our future in their clammy hands. If this were an Ikea delivery gone wrong, Mr B would have (very effectively) whooped their asses into gear without hesitation. But this? Something infinitely more important (and expensive) than a Billy Bookcase? Best not, eh? Don't want them to get pissed off with us or anything.

And so we wash down our outrage with another bottle of wine and look in the mirror and say, 'I AM ENTIRELY CONFIDENT IN A SUCCESSFUL OUTCOME. NO REALLY.

'NO.

'REALLY.'

9.

What is it like to meet your surrogate?

To understand what it is like to meet your surrogate, you first need to acquire said viable surrogate. A viable one. Not a maybe one or a potential one or a not suitable one, so yes. Months later, we match with Surrogate No. 3. It looks like this one is the one, and her name is ... oh God, sorry, that's my phone ringing, just hang on a moment please.

It's Lacey, the donor egg coordinator from The Agency. She's calling to deliver the news we've been waiting for with feverishly bated breath. Donor no. 234's cycle produced nineteen eggs, which is actually amazing. Eighteen of them fertilized with Mr B's sperm, which is totally fantastic – if a bit weird and slightly heart-wrenching. Someone else's eggs fertilised with my husband's sperm. Ew. It feels like cheating, on some kind of sub-clinical level. Like I wasn't enough, so he literally needed to go for a younger model. Anonymous, sure. Nameless, faceless even, but their biological matter made love in a petri dish in Miami and I ... ew ... I must try much harder not to think about it like that. That's the trick. Where was I? Oh yes, the big, breath-baiting news we need is how many survived the next five days to make it to blastocyst stage, and therefore viable embryos. How many? Well, we have to wait another five days it seems. This is just the first instalment of egg donor news. And there was me thinking we'd be cracking open the champagne and toasting our maybe-babies already. Goodness this process takes its time. But still, we have a potential surrogate! So, where was I?

Ah yes, her name is Melissa. And this is how it goes when it actually *goes*.

This time we know what to look for in the profile we're sent before we let out our breaths and excitedly clasp each other's hands on the sofa; Melissa has only had two children, and she doesn't want anymore. She has a perfectly clean bill of mental health, in fact she's done surrogacy once before, seven years ago for a woman in Denmark. Her administrative job is not the best or worst paid in the state of Illinois where she lives, and she and her husband Chad are really excited to meet us over Skype tomorrow at midnight. It sounds quite romantic, that. The stroke of midnight. But actually it's to accommodate the time difference, and we'll be chaperoned by Zoe, The Agency CEO, so in a way it feels like we're waiting for a highly emotional job interview to take place, digitally, and overseen by the big boss.

At three minutes to midnight it is suddenly VERY important to us that we have the right music on in the background. Nothing too definitive or alternative or with too much personality or— 'Just put my "dinner" playlist on,' says Mr B, who is himself really quite flustered, and agonising over whether to go to the loo now or hold it for however long this interview – sorry, meeting – is going to last. Dinner playlist? God no, way too jazzy. Opera? Intense. Um, um, Radiohead? Argh, sad. In the end we settle on nothing, because the laptop is ringing now, and there, when we press 'answer', are the gentle faces of Melissa and her husband Chad.

What do you even say? What's the appropriate intro to a four-way transatlantic conversation as unusual and consequential as this? We went for 'HI!!!!!' with the enthusiasm of five – count them – exclamation marks. It's difficult to gauge Chad and Melissa's response because their mouths are moving but no sound is coming out. There follows an agonizingly awkward few minutes of staccato mime before we establish that Melissa's volume isn't working and we need to regroup on a different device in a few minutes.

I can feel a panic attack edging at my subconscious, making me feel physically sick. I keep rationalising out loud, in an unconvincingly cheery voice while Mr B nods maniacally back at me. 'Why are we nervous? There's nothing to be nervous about. They'll like us. Surely. Won't they?'

Because this is the decider. The chips-down interview of interviews. *Will* we like each other? Will we want to proceed on this journey together, to go from transatlantic strangers to an intrinsically and emotionally linked four-some, forever (if we're being optimistic about how this will all end up).

The answer is yes before we've even heard their voices, because my goodness we've been waiting for such a long time already. There's nothing like repeated disappoint-ment, and rapidly increasing age, to make you superimpose your ideals on this new couple of saviours. My heart is full, and it must be blinding me, because I straight up ADORE Melissa already, purely for what she wants to do for us, and all I have to go on so far are her eyebrows (thick, impressive) and her husband (male, of indeterminate height).

They're back, squashed into her phone screen this time, and now we start, just by starting, really. Isn't that how all good friendships occur? There's no planning or faltering, it's just talking to each other. Being genuinely interested and enjoying the ease of the chat. Sure, yes, we have Zoe there, interjecting every so often, like a moder-ator on a panel discussion. 'So, guys, how about you tell Melissa and Chad a little bit about how you guys fell in love and what it is you guys love about each other.' But we really don't need her. We oscillate between these schmaltzy requests and deep existential chat (what it means to be a mother/how love makes a family), until we forget we're strangers chatting through a computer screen. I mean, these are the people who will carry and protect our baby – depending on how the rest of this process goes of course – and suddenly the surreality of this scenario hits me and I have to look away as I well up. For the first of five or six times that evening. It's the perfect halfway point between ecstatically happy and profoundly sad. I let Mr B chat with Chad while I sort my face out off screen.

He asks the fundamental question that we often ponder over ourselves: How does he feel about his wife being pregnant for someone else? Because honestly, it takes a special kind of person to be the supportive arm in this menagerie. Chad and Melissa only got married six months ago, yet he is fully supportive of her decision to have their first pregnancy for someone else. Why? 'I knew Melissa years ago when she did the first surrogacy and I saw how happy it made her, so why wouldn't I want her to be that happy again?'

Good point, well made. For Melissa, who says she is 'done' with having her own children, her reasoning is simple. She just loves being pregnant. Never happier, in fact, so acting as a surrogate pretty much provides the perfect solution, along with a healthy pay cheque of course. I'm glad that she's so open and honest about it. There is such a murky grey area around the moral implications of commercial surrogacy, and where there is money involved, there is always opportunity for exploitation. I need to understand the psychology behind putting oneself up for surrogacy in a country that allows payment for it, so that I can be truly comfortable with their circumstances and motivation. It's as vitally important for me – so that I can sleep at night (for the rest of my life) – as it should be for the good and caring clinics and agencies that facilitate this thing. I need to understand that the surrogates' motivation is sound, that they are in the right frame of mind going into it – and that they'll be able to cope well afterwards too. There are checks for that kind of thing, yes, but there's nothing like a face-to-face conversation to settle some spiking anxieties. And then we're done! We hang up and Mr B and I gaze at each other with sparkling eyes. This feels like the walk home from a very successful first date. The future is so full of promise and hope and, my God, we're so excited. There will definitely be no sleep happening tonight at least.

First off, the feeling was mutual. Apparently we spent the night thinking about them, and they about us, and lo, we now have an agreement to proceed. Which means progress. Ahh, sweet, sweet progress. But an agreement in America is not worth the intangible fluffy cloud it's conceived upon, and so we need to sort the next bit. The contract. No wait! First things first, we need to sort the medical, to see if we even need a contract. Jeez, there are a lot of steps that are really beginning to feel interminably long and protracted and, yes, expensive. Melissa lives in Chicago. She needs to fly to Dr Hernandez's clinic in Miami to have her medical. Until now, the only indication that Melissa is 'fit for the job' is that she put her hand up and volunteered. Having two children as well as acting as a surrogate years ago suggests that all will be fine, but as I very well know, human bodies can be wholly unreliable and throw a spanner in the works quietly and when you least expect it. The point of this initial medical is not only to make sure that Melissa is able to carry a baby, but to work out a treatment plan specific to her in order to make her uterus as welcoming as possible, on the exact right day they will schedule the transfer.

Before any of that can happen though, she also needs to be 'psychologically cleared', so yes we have another step to get through. I am grateful for the regulation surrounding this process in the States, though; it's a big part of why we chose to do it over there. And so I need to have a word with myself about how impatient I'm being because really, for me, the psychological part is perhaps the biggest and most important hurdle. I often worry about how my actions might have affected other people; and this is the mother of all affecting actions, if you'll excuse the pun. We are dealing with a highly emotive and complex issue here, plus this is a medical event and we all have a duty of care, so bring on the psych clearance so we can get on with the medical clearance and then the legal clearance. Anything I've left out there? Any other kind of clearance we need to clear? No?

A few days later and Melissa lets us know she passed the psychological test with bells on – of course she did! – and so we go over what the medical will entail.

I already know what her appointment will look like since I've been there very many times before myself. An ultrasound to take a big-picture look at her uterus and lining, then a hysteroscopy – a procedure using a tiny camera to take a much closer look inside the womb to check for abnormalities or underlying issues. Finally, a ton of blood tests to check for hormone levels, STDs, any other kinds of Ds, and then she's done.

Except we are really struggling to get any time or actually any response from the fertility clinic in Miami. Dr Hernandez was introduced to us by The Agency, so we try to get some help from them, who just do what we do and call and call and wait for a return call that never comes. The team might be brilliant (are they? I guess we'll find out), but they are notoriously slow at answering any phone call or email or simple question. And we have a lot of those. The time difference compounds things, sure, but even without that they take their sweet time with us.

That is, until we need to pay our package fee and sign the agreement. Then we can schedule the medical. It's all very conditional, but what do I know? Maybe this is how it works over there.

The payment they're after is for their enhanced fertility package that allows for four embryo transfers. That means that if it works the first time, we will have paid above the odds, but if it takes all four, we will have saved quite a lot of money, so we need to work out if this is the best way forward. Off the package, each embryo transfer alone costs about $15,000, which is staggeringly expensive, to me at least. Someone who has been through that very procedure five times in Russia, at around a twentieth of the cost. The whole thing takes five minutes or so and it's not unlike a smear test, in fact, just with more people in surgical scrubs and an ultrasound afterwards so you can see your little embryo lit up in your uterus. That definitely felt like an invaluable moment every time in Russia, but $9,500 extra to do it in the US? Um. No choice it seems.

So we sign the agreement and pay the package and, finally, finally book the medical appointment. Plus the flights for Melissa and Chad. Plus the hotel and hire car and childcare and insurance and top up the expenses account. I hate it when it feels this transactional, but it is what it is, right? In fact, I suppose that's exactly what it is, only most business agreements don't come hand in hand with very high emotional stakes on all sides. For my part, I am battling with so many conflicting feelings I don't know which one to concentrate on first, so I just let them float around my head a bit, obstructing my view and spiking my anxiety levels, and then bury them quickly, because that's easier, isn't it. Who wants to deal with a guilty conscience when considering their, well, their enlisting a stranger to do what their body cannot? Or a stubborn jealousy, or the remorse at the necessity of a stranger-replacement in the first place? Or a kind of disgust at the fact money has to change hands? Not me, thanks. I'd rather pretend emotions don't exist within my subconscious and just focus on the practical. Practical, practical, practical, la-di-da. Di-da.

*   *   *

Mr B and I are sat at home thinking hard about Melissa at her medical. Willing her to have as fabulous a time as such an appointment allows, and it all to go brilliantly well. It's the least we all deserve, surely.

So far this morning she's kept up a regular text chat, keeping us up to date on everything, from how comfortable her hotel bed was (not at all, unfortunately) to how long she's been kept waiting in the waiting room (an inordinately long time, unfortunately), so I'm really working hard over here, trying to suppress the guilt and the worry, and did I mention the guilt?

But Melissa's been quiet for quite a bit now, so we assume she's finally having her appointment. Exciting! This is the first mega hurdle and it's being cleared as we speak. It's so crazy to think there is a team in a whole other continent assessing how best to create our baby, right now! Mr B and I sit in silence and try to conjure up good news by staring hard at the phone screen.

Nothing.

Still nothing.

BRRRRIIIIING! No caller ID. It's her! It's her! Oh my heart, no one rings with good news anymore, is she calling to say it's all off? 'Hello?' I whisper.

It's not her. It's Lacey, egg donor coordinator. She's dropped us a line to let us know that of our eighteen embryos, only five developed adequately for the PGD testing. Remember, that security blanket that involves taking a tiny single-cell biopsy from the day-five blastocysts to test for any abnormalities or genetic diseases, so that you know you're transferring the chromosomally 'normal' ones back. This reduces the risk of miscarriage and increases the chance of implantation. At this point, although it's yet another thing that costs yet more money, it's an investment-worthy no-brainer for us. But of course, it takes more time.

And according to Lacey, we only have five to biopsy.

Well, this feels like a blow. The thought of so many potential embryos not making it is really quite sad. Try as I might, I can't help humanising them, even before they're viable. Of course, we were hoping for more day-five blastocysts after our seemingly strong start. More chance of receiving good news about how many will make it to 'normal' status. So now we need to hope they all test well.

'Your chromosomal analysis results should be ready in a few weeks,' she says, before she signs off.

Well today is stressful. I resume my position of phone-screen-staring and good-news-willing until:

PING! A message. It's Melissa this time.

That was a rather rough appt as far as 'exams' go. He said I have a cyst on my ovary, which he has to try to shrink, so I have another appointment in 4–6 weeks to see if it's OK to proceed.

Well. Um. The aim of the game is to fill Melissa with positivity. There's no room for feeling like she might have let us down in any way because, whilst we do feel let down – very much so at this point – it's absolutely not with her. More at the universe. Fucking universe. What more does it want from me?

> OK Melissa, that's great! You're on your way home, cysts are totally normal and it'll resolve really soon, please try not to worry. Are you OK?

I'm very good at all of the above, but I'm thankful this conversation is veiled by the fact it's text chat, so she can't see my sad face.

> Very uncomfortable and will be for a few days, but that's all part of the pregnancy process.

This is when I look within myself and summon the resources to not spike at the (hopefully unintentional, but still) guilt-inducing content of the message. I will not feel jealous that I cannot know any part of the pregnancy process myself. I will not, I … I don't have those resources yet. Jeez I feel bad.

The next couple of weeks we spend checking in on Melissa and worrying about how much we're worrying. Whenever it all feels totally out of my control (which is every day, to be honest), I find it easiest to just shake it out of my head and stop thinking. Like an irresponsible child. But the waiting is nearly as stressful as attempting to manage the process from the other side of the world.

We want to book in the next appointment to reassess the cyst situation, but we are having very little luck. Again. We have our mediators – The Agency – who are supposed to keep us posted on the clinic, or help us communicate with them at the very least. And who tell us every time we check in that this amount of waiting and lack of clinic contact is completely normal. And then we become mediators ourselves, relaying the information to the understandably antsy Melissa and Chad, who tell us the opposite.

I take on the role of pacifier, 'Try not to worry Mel, I'm assured by The Agency it's totally normal. Is it not totally normal?'

But Melissa has danced this dance once before, remember. So she's all, 'Oh gracious, NO. I know this is NOT how things typically run. The last time everything was like clockwork.'

Great.

Shit.

When we still haven't heard about when or whether we can proceed, or even about the number of embryos we have to proceed with, I try Jane, The Agency coordinator, one more time. And I receive an out-of-office message.

I will be travelling to the fertility clinic for my transfer. I will be back to work on Wednesday, but working from home so that I can rest. Enjoy your day!

For your transfer? Jane? I can safely assume, since we are all working within the parameters of infertility language here, that she is talking about an embryo transfer. I stare at the message for a while, wondering why I suddenly feel so uncomfortable. Either she's trying for her own baby, needs IVF and is OK with letting anyone who emails know about her specific cycle timings, or our surrogacy coordinator is going to be a surrogate herself. Tomorrow. I'm struggling to fathom why she didn't tell us, because whilst it's technically none of our business, business-wise, it feels like it is. This presents a conflict of interest, surely? Might she not be able to get direct and timely answers from our doctor or clinic because she's concentrating on facilitating her own surrogacy journey? Could she have lost some focus perhaps? We already know from the massive hassle of doing it ourselves, that acting as a surrogate is full-on, emotionally and physically. And also, am I envious that everyone round here seems to be getting pregnant except Melissa, and me? Abso-bloody-lutely.

I can't do anything about it. She hasn't broken any laws, but she hasn't done an awful lot for us thus far either, so whilst I reaffirm my niggling worry that we maybe went with the wrong agency for this life-changing event, I did it of my own volition. It's nobody's fault but mine, so I just need to get on with facilitating this thing myself. I say 'I', I mean 'Mr B', since he is the one taking the brunt of the legwork off mine (and Jane's) hands.

Lo and behold, days later he has managed to bypass every usual avenue, and got hold of Dr Hernandez himself. Melissa is having her follow-up appointment as we speak, so we're waiting – again – for the all-important message that piques our anticipatory anxiety, and lets us know whether or not we can proceed as this wonder team of four. So can we?

We have completed the biopsy of your embryos …

Oh! This is the other bit of news we've been waiting for. If it doesn't rain, it pours, eh? An egg-donor email from Lacey about the results of our pre-genetic diagnostics to eliminate any chromosomal abnormalities that would compromise a successful transfer. AKA, how many embryos do we have in the freezer?

We have three.

Only three. It feels like a blow. Three embryos ultimately means just three chances of success. It sets a limit for us that I badly wanted to be bigger. If being disappointed with that sounds greedy, having personally tried and failed so many times before, three seems tiny. To put it into context, when I did my donor-egg IVF in Russia we had six embryos. Six chances. Also, our financial 'package' with the fertility clinic is based on four embryo transfers, which means we've paid for one chance that will never be used. So yes, whilst I keep telling myself having three 'perfect' embryos is absolutely not bad news, it definitely could be better.

There is a mantra that comes in quite handy at this point, and it is uttered up and down the country by well-meaning fertile people to their infertile friends, who suppress an inward snarl of contempt. (Infertile to infertile is OK though, because it's true.)

'It only takes one'.

I have a good friend who, after years of trying naturally, saved enough money for one round of IVF. Her treatment resulted in one embryo. One. It managed to make it to day five, when they had their one-chance transfer and put it back in. I cannot imagine the terrible pressure of the next two weeks, waiting for the results of that one and only pregnancy test. I pick up my phone to ask her exactly what that was like, and then remember she's on the holiday of a lifetime with her husband and their gorgeous seven-year-old daughter. Miraculous, eh? It only takes one.

So here we are. We've remortgaged our home and we have three rolls of the dice to deliver an extra person to take up space in it. So thanks for letting us know Lacey, I need to go and percolate a little. And wait for Melissa's medical clearance. I need to go and drink a little, actually. Whisky should do it. Where was I?

Ah yes, Melissa's follow-up ultrasound report has come through – finally – and it shows that, drumroll please, Melissa's cyst has gone! That means we have medical clearance! Which means for the first time in five long months, we can say we officially have a surrogate. And, would you believe, a treatment schedule and a tentative embryo transfer date. This is when it starts to feel exciting. This is when, try as you might, you can't stop fantasising about your future baby toddling round the side of the sofa, because in six short weeks we should know whether our first transfer achieved a pregnancy. Oh. My. Gosh!

The medical protocol for an IVF cycle involves daily oestrogen tablets to plump the lining of the womb, make it nice and welcoming for a passing embryo to embed within. Then, later, progesterone injections to support the perfectly plumped endometrium. So there are some definite hormonal side effects floating around and I'm trying to tell myself these are the reasons for Melissa's increasingly odd attitude towards me. Or maybe it's that we're largely communicating on WhatsApp, and perhaps her tone is lost in translation? Am I being too sensitive because I'm sort of left out now? I can say this here, and only here, but I kind of feel like I'm in a declining relationship with a boy and I'm trying hard to convince him not to leave me. Which is no sort of analogy to explain the complex beauty of surrogacy, surely? But she keeps telling me how put out she is by everything, like the annoying journey to the drugstore to pick up the meds. Or how big the needle is and how much she knows it's going to hurt. The thing is, I know how much it hurts because I've stabbed myself with the exact same one exactly fifty-four times in my own quest to get pregnant, and it's really not bad once you get your head around puncturing your own flesh. But even so, I feel terrible whenever she tells me how bad she's feeling on my behalf.

And then there are the expenses. Every trip Melissa and Chad take of course incurs expenses, which come to us through The Agency, and which we, of course, need to cover. When Mr B and I went to Miami to meet Dr Hernandez and make The Deposit, we did the taxi journey from the airport where the window sticker says 'there is a flat 45 dollar fare for any airport journey'. So then, why did we get two 90 dollar airport taxi expense claims, with lost receipts? Or a loss of earnings claim for both she and Chad, who went with her for the one-night round-trip scan, requiring childcare, which came to 500 dollars apparently.

Is that OK, or …? Anyone advise me on whether I need to start worrying? Anyone? I'm quickly learning that being the Intended Parent is an exercise in self-restraint. Right now, I have to disregard my feelings for the greater good. I am probably paranoid about the expenses, and I need to have a word with myself. Trust is as big a part of this game as science. Because even with a contract, Melissa could back out at any point before a confirmed pregnancy. And really, just because my sensitivities and feelings are so present for me all the time, it doesn't mean they are for anyone else. Why would Melissa think for a moment that her natural commentary on feeling anxious about an injection might twang a nerve in me more painful than the needle in her bum? I suppose she's focused on her own journey as much as I am focused on mine. We want to and will do everything in our power to make this woman feel good about what she's doing for us. It's instinctive. We want her to be happy because we are positively swimming in gratitude. So yeah, it's (probably) not her, it's me; I'm so used to being let down by now, plus this whole concept is still so alien to me. I massively respect and admire anyone who could put themselves up for carrying someone else's baby. But I guess I still can't believe I'm the someone else.

And since we're being real, we need her more than she needs us. Right now, it feels as though Melissa could tell me she finds my face hard to look at, and I'd apologise profusely and put it down to the hormones. But – argh! I can't help it – it's niggling me because it feels like Melissa knows that too.

They say that, as long and painful as surrogacy or IVF can sometimes feel, once it gets going it really goes at a pace. And, I can't believe I'm writing this down, everything so far (medically at least) has gone exactly how it needed to go. The scans have been brilliant. Relying on news of someone else's uterine lining thickening up nicely has been surreal. Melissa seems a little warmer with every bit of positive progress, and the transfer is scheduled for next week! Next week!

And then.

Something is wrong.

Not a text I relish receiving, but there it is nonetheless, practically pulsating in my inbox.

It's from Melissa, which makes it even worse. The all-important last scan before the transfer has shown a large collection of fluid in her uterus. Trying to achieve a successful embryo transfer now would be like dropping an ant in the middle of a swimming pool and hoping it somehow makes it to the side. I can't believe it. Unfortunately we now need to ask Melissa to have the fluid drained, and hope we can still go ahead as planned. I feel like I'm about to destabilise a canoe that we've finally got to float, and relationship-wise, I'm pretty sure that is not the place to be at this point. I don't know how to make it better, or more mutually appreciative maybe, so I stick with what I know – abject kindness. Soon she's the other side of the appointment and our doctor tells us it worked! He drained most of the fluid, plus the progesterone she is due to take between now and the transfer would likely dry up the rest. The transfer is back on. Jubilant, excited, feeling as though we've swerved a bullet, we send Melissa all the thumbs-ups, WOOHOOs and how are you feelings that we can type at once. The two blue ticks come up to say she's read them and then …

OK.

I don't know what to do with this despondency. I don't think I deserve it, in fact, and if I'm being honest with myself, it's starting to make me a little bit mad. Surrogacy is a hugely emotional experience, and one that you generally reach at the end of an already emotional ride. This much is obvious. I'd imagine this is also what spurs most people on to sign up for surrogacy in the first place, to help. I already had a hunch, but now I'm coming to realise there are so many weird and complex feelings involved: jealousy, admiration, fear, anxiety, trust, mistrust. Having a positive and open relationship with the person helping you to get there can only help to alleviate some of the more difficult feelings, right? So why don't we have one? Why does this feel so difficult?

Things don't particularly improve in the lead-up to our embryo transfer day, but not for want of trying. I'm determined that Melissa will never get a hint of how I'm really feeling – how she's making me feel. That is my commitment, to reframe my pessimism and, OK, yes, potential paranoia about her attitude, assume it is lost in translation. Bury my anxieties basically and smile. Always smile! And what is there not to smile about? We're taking the first of our three chances and investing it in Melissa. Quite literally speaking. It's happening today in fact.

I wait till an acceptable hour to message her, taking the time difference into account. She'll have woken up in a hotel in Miami with her husband, Chad, by her side. They'll probably be having breakfast about now.

So much good luck to us all today! I hope you're feeling OK?

There is no response. SMILE! SMILE, smile smile, smi—
This is killing me.

This is such a big day for us all, but I'm actually being shut out of it and it's killing me. Doesn't she know? Can't she imagine how I must be feeling right now, at home in London? I'm so far removed, physically, literally, geographically, and it hits me, again, that I am the one member of this party of four that has zero involvement in this. Therefore I can only hope that Melissa wants to bring me in, otherwise I'm just someone who has paid for a medical procedure that's about to occur, and that's about it. How uncomfortable and true and upsetting is that?

After four hours – *four hours* – of postulating and agonising and reasoning with myself and Mr B, I try again.

Are you doing OK, lovely? What time is the appointment again?

I know when it is, of course I do, I just don't have anything else to say.

Melissa is typing ... (Oh, thank Christ.)

It was 11 but they want me in earlier so I'm on my way.

It occurs to me that this kind of news would have been nice to be offered rather than extracted, but that's paranoid, pessimistic me talking, right? So instead – Hooray!

On their way to the clinic for what we can only hope will be the one and only embryo transfer.

What do you do when someone is off in a whole other continent being impregnated on your behalf? You do very little but sit and percolate, that's what. There are so many layers to get through, so many surreal complications and scenarios that have brought us to this point. Us two, sat in our south London kitchen, waiting to hear how our collective embryo transfer went, before we then wait another two weeks to see how it *really* went. It's something like nervous excitement but that doesn't really do it justice either. Positive and negative stress crammed into the same heart chamber. Must remember to breathe.

Right now our embryo is being prepared to become *someone*. How profoundly, utterly amazing! We think like this, with a fizz in our chests for about an hour.

And then, again, Melissa is typing ...

Have you spoken to the doctor? I'm a mess.

I go cold. I daren't look at my husband who, sure enough, just picked up the phone to Dr Hernandez. They did a scan (3,000 dollars) before they began to thaw the frozen embryo, thank goodness, because the fluid has returned with a vengeance and he recommends that we stop. Stop this transfer, stop this cycle, stop our connection with Melissa, full stop. She 'most likely isn't a viable surrogate'.

Apparently this kind of anomaly happens and there is no way of predicting or preparing for it, but the doctor suggests we start looking for another surrogate. Unfathomable. OK, our relationship could be better, the communication needs some work, but we've come so far already! There are such complicated logistics and so much cost associated with every part of the search. We're supposed to be doing a pregnancy test in two weeks, for goodness' sake! This whole long process has been like a labour in itself.

We have two options at this point. Start the search for another surrogate along with all of the legal, medical and financial burden that presents or, if she is willing, try one more IVF cycle with Melissa, because there is a chance the fluid build-up was a one-off and next time it might be fine. 'It will be a lot quicker and less expensive for you if it works out with Melissa,' he says, but it's a gamble and he doesn't have any idea what our odds look like.

'To be perfectly honest, it's rare enough that I haven't seen enough cases to make a comparable judgment.' Of course it is. This is us we're talking about.

After a stiff drink and a solid cry, I remember my commitment to support Melissa, first and foremost, and send a message:

Hey Melissa. I think we are all three a bit deflated, so just reaching out to say keep your chin up and let's see what the next few weeks bring and go from there. Please, please don't worry and please take care of yourself.

She doesn't reply to say she hopes we are feeling OK, to recognise our pain too, or to check in on us. She doesn't reply to say she will try to keep her chin up, or even with a misguided attempt to apologise. In fact, she doesn't reply at all.

10.

What is it like to lose your surrogate?

I think I'm being ghosted. I think my surrogate is ghosting me. Melissa is doing such an excellent job of ending this particular relationship by suddenly and without explanation withdrawing from all communication, that we now only speak to Jane, our surrogacy coordinator. And this is the case right now, that we are preparing to – maddeningly – go ahead with a second IVF cycle with Melissa. In the hope that we can go ahead with the second attempt at the first embryo transfer. Confused? Not as much as me, don't worry.

The thought of doing this again with her, but without her talking to us, is incredibly uncomfortable. Have I done something wrong? Does she not like us anymore, in which case why is she happy to go ahead and try and get pregnant for us again? What the hell will the next nine months be like, will we need to enlist Jane as mediator for the whole time? This is incredibly depressing and I feel totally stuck. Completely undone. I have no idea what to do, so we just blindly press ahead. I have a strong feeling that this is not going to be so OK, but right now, what other choice do we have?

There's another mission we need to complete before we can get going, too, because it's at this point that we need to think about the law again. Sigh. Because it's these bureaucratic bits that really bring it home for me. We need to hire attorneys for goodness' sake, loads of them, it seems, to what, negotiate our baby making? It's another part of this unusual process that feels so transactional, so impersonal. But it's time to get our ducks in as neat a row as possible, and so our US attorney, Carla, has put us in touch with a London law firm to handle the UK side of things. I was naive to this fact when we started out in the States. I thought by going there we just sort of skip over England and its out-of-date surrogacy legalities. But apparently not; we need to put our US and UK lawyers in touch, so we take Carla's advice and connect with her British peers. First we do some googling. The office of this particular family law firm is fancy, to say the least. The website is beautiful, the mahogany is prolific, these guys clearly have some reputable welly.

When we get off the train on the day of our appointment and amble down the central London street to the office hand in hand, I say this: 'Funny that we're going to the fanciest London law firm when all they have to do is a bit of red tape, eh?'

Mr B agrees, but it seems there isn't a huge pool of surrogacy lawyers in the British legal system, so we took Carla's recommendation at face value and it seems like the right thing to do. 'Just don't get carried away and start thinking we need the top dogs just 'cos they've got a nice office,' I said.

And that's the last time I remember smiling that day.

Having never been to a lawyer in my adult life, I am pretty much 100 per cent naive, but I assume the expression of someone who knows who they're dealing with. I'm well-practised from every MOT I've taken my car in for. We wait in the enormous waiting room – it is bigger than the entire footprint of my house – until we are collected and steered into another room twice the size. We're invited to sit at a humongous executive desk opposite three people, *Apprentice*-style, and I feel tiny.

The lawyer we are meeting, whom we'll call Theresa, begins, head tilted, asking us how we met, with a deeply sensitive expression. I start off thinking it is lovely, a getting to know you ice-breaker, but she asks more and more questions until it becomes a little uncomfortable. We just met for goodness' sake. She wants details. At this point I'm struggling to understand why it's important, and I chastise Mr B for waffling. He is definitely one for too much sentimental detail. I tell him off too often for it because it's sweet, really. I just don't want to waste these expensive people's time.

'No, no,' Theresa gently chastises me in return. 'It's vitally important we make a really strong case for your relationship to the High Court. We need to convince them that you're a solid parental unit, so intricate details are imperative.'

Holy what now? A strong case? The High Court? I'm not sure what the hell is happening because we just need to change some names on a birth certificate in nine months or so, no?

Um, in a word, no.

When we joined our American agency, there was a tiny moment where we touched upon the subject of a UK lawyer at the end of the whole process to formalise our parental responsibility once we got home. Then, when we appointed our first US attorney, she reiterated once again that we'd need a parental order in England, but that was literally the extent of the conversation. No one ever went into any more detail. So OK, we thought, that's something that happens at the end, and we mentally squirrelled a budget of two extra grand, as extra, extra contingency, on Mr B's Surrogacy Spreadsheet, and didn't think of it again. Until now.

Theresa sees me floundering, looks painfully sympathetic and continues: 'It's so lucky you came to us at this point because many intended parents leave it far too late. We need to get you an immigration lawyer *immediately* to advise on how best to bring your baby safely into this country. You'll need to be in the States for two to three months to get everything in order; if you don't do it properly, they could take your baby away at border control.'

We've been in the room for about ten minutes and it is already spinning. Three months is vastly different to the two weeks we were advised by our agency. We have lives!

We have jobs! And cats! And an ever-decreasing source of limited funds! How are we supposed to live in another country for a quarter of the year? I'm not prepared for that! I immediately start crying. Ahh yes, it's panic settling in, hello old friend.

The conversation went on in this vein for two hours. And I literally cried the whole time. My tears got fatter and faster and more embarrassing the whole time, but I couldn't stop. This feels so unfair and so unexpected.

By the end of it we had basically established that in doing this commercial process in the US, to escape our own archaic laws, we are flouting those laws as British citizens. If we intend to come back home and be parents here, then we have to convince the High Court that what we just did was OK. That process takes up to a year apparently, around three court appearances, reams of paperwork, a specialist QC, a specialist family lawyer, an immigration lawyer and a solid gold partridge in a pear tree. With a diamond-encrusted collar.

Theresa finished with a flourish, with the kicker to end all kickers. In response to Mr B's throat-clearing, ahem, price inquiry for this long, protracted, scary process, she nods with closed eyes and tells us, 'You two have been through hell. It's not fair, you've been treated appallingly and it's time someone looked after you properly. I want to be that person, because you need hand-holding. That level of service will cost in the region of £50,000.'

I stare at her. Fifty thousa-wuh?

'Plus VAT,' she finishes.

If I was crying before, I'm not sure what to call the snivelling mess I was in by the time I left Theresa's office.

We're stood outside bereft, utterly convinced we need this level of specialist care and utterly desolate that we can in no way afford it. Mr B has to hold me still because I'm shaking with racking sobs. So, now what? We are stuck. It honestly feels like we've basically been tricked into a surrogacy journey that we were never going to be able to complete.

It was only once I got home and called my mum that the anger set in. 'Darling, if they were taking babies away from people at the borders, we would have heard about it by now. How does anyone else manage to do international surrogacy? She was scaremongering.'

And my mum is right. Surely we can't be the first IPs in the world to have the rug pulled from under their feet this far down the line? There are countless numbers of international surrogacy successes that don't get stuck on this part of the story, surely. Or we would have heard about them by now.

It's true that the parental order process is exponentially more difficult this way round, because we're also trying to repatriate a whole new person. It's true that the High Court needs to hear our case and, therefore, because of all this extra red tape, it will cost thousands of pounds versus the £125 it costs to obtain a DIY parental order in the case of a UK surrogacy arrangement. It's true you need a lawyer, and a specialised one at that, but you definitely don't need to be scared into investing in the top end. You should be able to make that decision based on your finances, not your fear factor.

Help! SOS! Heeeeeelp!

Mercifully we were sent help in the form of a second opinion. (Moral of the story, always get a second opinion.) Fortuitously, our friend Billie introduces us to Vardags, a family law firm with a track record in fertility and surrogacy law. It confirms that, while it is going to be expensive – such is the nature of international surrogacy arrangements – it doesn't have to be quite *that* expensive. The lovely owner Ayesha tells us that the problem often arises this far down the line because there is a huge difficulty in the disparity between the laws around surrogacy in our two countries that no one talks about. No one. Understandably, not the US agencies who recruit international clients because, for one, and probably in our case, they simply don't know about them. Or else they don't want to put their prospective clients off. And then there are the US lawyers, who are so specialised in their individual state laws that they don't know the law in the next-door state, let alone a whole other continent. Ayesha is going to help us to do everything we now know we need, but for a fraction of the cost. In fact, she wants to lead a campaign to get the laws changed here, so more people don't suffer this same experience. Now you're talking; she is exactly my kind of woman. This feels like serendipity, it feels like a lifeline. The next stage of course is to actually get pregnant on the next cycle, so we can hopefully get to find out just how difficult this legal issue will become.

I feel like things are clicking into place the more good parts of this process we get ticked off. I know it isn't ever going to be easy, but I would love everything to be nice, at least. To be calm and kind. I keep thinking of Melissa and what possible reason she could have for withdrawing to this extent, and I suddenly reframe it all in my head. She must feel the weight of the world on her shoulders, she must feel terrible that it's got to the stage that we somehow only speak through a third party, surely. So I will rectify that. I will reach out again and show her how nice and calm and kind this thing can be. We're on the precipice of making this wonderful story a reality, and in a way we're all so lucky to get to live it. I decide I'm going to write her a meaningful note tomorrow that will get us all back on track. I'm determined that she's going to go into this next cycle refreshed, recalibrated and reminded that we're all good people and we care about each other. Without Jane mediating.

Oh no, wait! Scrap that. I just heard from Jane, Melissa has had another scan (how did we not know this?), and yep, it looks like the fluid is there again. Which means we finally have something in common, at last: neither of our bodies are compatible with pregnancy. Aka, Melissa cannot act as ours, or anyone else's surrogate. I feel bad for her, the woman has basically gone into this trying to help an infertile couple, and has ended it with her own infertility diagnosis. But at the same time, I'm questioning her motivation and licking my emotional wounds. I'm not alone here, am I? That whole thing didn't feel right, right? Jane is gracious enough to concede that Melissa's attitude towards us has been totally unacceptable: 'It's not how we would expect a surrogate to behave.'

I'm very much wondering how it is that we've landed here, six months after signing up for surrogacy with The Agency. Our third unsuitable surrogate, but this one has fallen through well into the race, just as we were about to pass the baton after the first leg in fact. Which means we were heavily invested. Emotionally, even though things weren't ideal. OK, things were a thousand miles from ideal – I was invested in the outcome. I imagined it happening with Melissa, I was spurring us on to get through the rough patch, and I'm told it's quite common for rough patches to occur. Particularly when things aren't going so well medically. The surrogate can feel a sense of guilt that might cause them to distance themselves from the intended parents. Which I totally get, but ghosting? Nuh uh. I said it quietly and shamefully to Mr B when no one else was looking, but at times Melissa made me feel like I was her PA. Like I was inconveniencing her by changing an appointment date, due to the meds not taking full effect yet. ('I've had to explain to work why I need to move my afternoon off and I'm not happy.') Or asking me at one in the morning to call the doctor in the States to ask a question for her because she didn't want to. If I was feeling that way before we even started, if I'm really honest with myself, it's better that we end things here. There's no way that imbalance in a relationship would have been sustainable for another nine months. I couldn't bear a cloud of negativity or doubt over what will be such a precious pregnancy. One day. So yes, I do feel bad for us, for her, for all sorts of reasons, but let me say this because it's what I'm thinking: it's worse for us. Dr Hernandez assures us that Melissa is healthy and happy. We on the other hand are heartbroken and hopeless. And straight up broke.

There is a cost to this particular loss, and it is astronomical. It is heartbreakingly wasteful. It is *coughs into hand* around £26,000. Down the toilet.

Mr B and I have spent the last few days spiralling. Lamenting the loss of Melissa, of the fact that we'd got so far logistically. We had medical clearance, which comes with it's own American private healthcare system fees. We'd gone through legal clearance, with an attorney each, and each with high 'billables'. We'd paid our $5,000 'match fee' to The Agency. All of Melissa's medications, the scans, the blood tests, the travel to and from each appointment, by plane and car and taxi, all the expenses. So I sat and wrote them all down in an attempt to tether ourselves back to earth a bit. Thinking it wouldn't be quite as bad as we were imagining, surely. And the grand total was £26,000. Needless to say, no one here feels better after that particular exercise.

And the even scarier thing is, since we're being quite blatantly open about our finances here, we've remortgaged the house twice already, because with the medical package and the hidden extras and the insurances and whatnot, all in all we've surpassed the 'worst case scenario' cost that The Agency laid out to us at the beginning. We've spent more than £90,000 and ... and ... we haven't even started yet. I know this because Mr B has been diligently and wonderfully keeping on top of the budget and logistics management like nobody's business. Again. I'm not entirely sure what use The Agency is to us when we have someone like him on the team. It's two in the morning – argh, time difference! – and he runs through his immaculate budget spreadsheet with Zoe, The Agency CEO, who initially gave us the timeline and the fee breakdown. He ran through it with her twice, because really Zoe, those numbers do not add up. And I really can't stress this enough – we *haven't even started yet*. Zoe starts off by looking at his final figure and reassuring us, 'No, that can't be right. Let's go over everything again.' So they do, and at the end she pauses a moment before telling us, verbatim: 'Well gee, guys, I'm so sorry. I guess it's more expensive than I thought.'

I can't.

I can't even.

It is so clear to see how easy it is to get into terribly difficult financial situations when it comes to this route to parenthood. And it is becoming increasingly clear that there are plenty of people willing to take advantage of that. We knew about the basics when we started: the surrogate fee, the agency, the doctor and medical package, the legal stuff and the insurance and medication, but doctors' fees vary wildly depending on where you go. We've discovered that ours, as recommended by The Agency, charges almost double what most others would. But then there are the hidden extras that crop up along the way. Every week with Melissa would bring another email from The Agency asking for her 'extra fees'. It turns out there's a compensation cost associated with every step of the process and the surrogate can essentially choose what she asks for. On top of the cost of the medication, for example, is compensation for starting to take the medication, at $500. There is compensation for having the embryo transfer procedure – $500. Compensation for having a caesarean section would be $5,000. There are various others outlined in the contract, the worst of which is compensation for having a miscarriage, at $500. This of course has mental health and physical trauma implications for anyone who suffers one, no matter if they are carrying their own baby or someone else's. But it seems such an oddity to put a figure on it. We would lose everything in that terrible instance, but we'd have to pay extra for the pleasure. But we also both know it is impossible to stop, because then this will all have been for nothing. I think I can cope with spending all this money – our future child's inheritance – on its own existence, but there has to be a child in the end because the more we spend trying to make it happen, the more we stand to throw away if we decide to stop, and then I know can't cope. I won't ever be able to sleep again for the twisting agony of all that emotional and financial investment for nothing. So then, what? We beg, borrow and find money to keep going and keep going until we win? Isn't that how gambling addiction is perceived? Is that what is happening here?

I don't want to think like this. I want to shake every frightening, tainted thought from my head. The only thing for it is to make a plan. I need progress in order to feel OK right now, it's the only way I work. I need to forget about losing Melissa, and the fact we just flushed the best part of a year's salary down the loo, and move forward. So, um, how? Please?

OK, so this is the direction my addled brain takes: like a large percentage of the population, I'm still not *quite* sure where we are on the legality or otherwise of cannabis. Specifically hash cookies. It was not OK, and then it was for a bit, then it really wasn't again, except medicinally, I think? But anyway, this doesn't have much to do with anything, except this one time when it *really* does.

For the record, I cannot do drugs. I literally cannot even 'do' citalopram, an anti-anxiety medication that I was prescribed following my cancer diagnosis. I got every one of the rare side effects, that – at its worst point – required an ambulance to come to my home at one in the morning. I couldn't do drugs when I tried my first puff of a friend's joint in my teens and had an alarming whitey in their parents' toilet. And as such I don't and haven't touched the green stuff since. You see? I didn't even know what colour it actually is.

My friend Anna has invited me to a dinner party to try and take my mind off my worries. I definitely don't feel like going, but in the spirit of life-living and positive thinking, I drag myself there, albeit late. I don't know this person who's answered the door, but she's a wonderfully bubbly character, wearing a floaty dress and a leafy wreath on her head, and she immediately offers me a hash cookie she's baked and brought with her. Oh! Um … This is not a situation I have often found myself in as an adult. As a teenager, yes. I likely would have taken one to look cool, and then hurled it away like a lit stick of dynamite at the first available second. But as a grown-up?

I politely decline, 'Oh no, NO no no no, thank you though, but no.' And we end up having a totally lovely evening with definitely much more notable giggling than you'd expect at a dinner party. It's exactly the kind of evening I wish I could have all the time, with no over-thinking or sad undertones or any other rubbish side effects that come with years' worth of cancer-in-duced-infertility-related anxiety. And it makes me think. And then it's with some surprise that I find myself lingering on the doorstep as I leave, quietly asking for a hash-cookie doggie bag. The monumental, insomnia-fuel-ling, constant, aggravating, exhausting, insurmountable stress of this specific situation, is making me want to be baked, unfazed, permanently positive.

This is my thinking: *These smart, grown-up women have clearly had a great time; they're themselves, only slightly more fun, and maybe I could just have a nice, chilled moment. Maybe I could sink into my sofa and feel blissful and relaxed, but in the safety and comfort of my own home, with my husband to protect me.* And also, and this was my crucial error: *OK, so I know I can't smoke this stuff, but a chocolate chip cookie? That's entry level, right?'*

WRONG. Resolutely, reliably – trust me – wrong.

Evil malady disguised as sweet baked goods is the evilest kind of evil if you ask me. I got home and nibbled a tiny bit, sunk into the sofa and waited for … well, nothing. So then, because it was as good if not better than a classic Maryland cookie, I ate half. I watched an entire episode of *Dragons' Den* with not so much as a tingle in my toes, and then I went to bed and fell asleep easily, something that has been eluding me for quite some time.

Ahh, the sweet sleep of the intoxicated: super-chilled, uninterrupte— Oh wait, I need a wee! So I get up, with my eyes half closed as I do every time I need to pee in the night because it helps you stay in the sleepiest sleep-state possible. I sit down on the loo, I do my thing, except I'm also somehow outside the room at the same time. Am I, wait, am I … hallucinating? My heart is immediately grand-prix-racing, and oh! I can't feel my face. I stumble back into bed and try to calm down because I know a severe panic attack when I feel one. OK THIS, this is entirely different, but IT's STILL feeling like PANIC, just MUCH WOrse thAn NORMaL, just BREaTHE. Breathing will help. I wait until my heart is definitely about to stop all together, and then I frantically claw at Mr B to wake him up, whispering urgently, 'HELP ME, please help me, something is wrong. I need help, please.'

He immediately diagnoses me as 'totally stoned', and even though this will eventually turn out to be true and then, because it is true, funny, right now it absolutely is not. I was very seriously ill once, so I am now a high-functioning hypochondriac. My mind loses its ability to be rational about my health, so that I freak out when I have a simple cold because it reminds me of how really sick I once was. So, this totally out of control feeling taking over my body? This is worse than anything that came before it. I have absolute confidence I'm about to die. I need someone with the right equipment to be able to resuscitate me at any moment. So WHY is Mr B holding off from pressing go on the 999 call?

'Are you sure babe?' he says. 'It's just the hash cookie, you just need to calm down.'

Again, retrospectively, it's obvious that he pretty much knows I'll be OK, and so he is reluctant to get the authorities involved. His wife has just ingested illegal drugs, after all. Not to me though, nope, my husband is quite clearly trying to kill me. He is holding off calling the ambulance to finish me off the easy way.

By now it's totally physical. I'm gasping for breath, losing the ability to talk and amazed my blood is still contained in my body, because my heart is trying so hard to pump it out onto the floor.

I make him drive me, at half two in the morning, to A&E. I make him jump four red lights because I know for a fact that if we stop, I won't make it. And once I'm triaged, it, um, turns out there is nothing wrong with me, and, erm, it *was* just the cookie after all. Then, only after I've come down in the waiting room, the embarrassingly young, justifiably pissed-off doctor who finally sees me at five in the morning takes the opportunity to shame me loudly in front of everyone: 'WE OFFER A REFERRAL SERVICE TO DRUG ABUSERS. DO YOU WANT ME TO REFER YOU?'

I still think that was a bit much. Granted, I've massively wasted time he could have used to save someone's life, but I absolutely thought I was that someone at that point. Such is the terrible, stupid irresponsibility of taking stupid drugs. Maybe refer me, doc. I'm sorry.

By the time he saw me I was coherent, ashamed and over the worst. 'I don't do drugs, this isn't me, we've been having a really hard time recently. I just wanted to feel better for a little bit.' He just rolled his eyes, felt my glands and sent me home.

The saddest part (in every sense of the word) is that I've been thinking I was OK this whole time. I'd like to gently suggest to myself at this point that maybe this three-day turnaround for mental recovery that I've come to think of as my resilience superpower, is less miraculous, more avoidant. I suspect I'm just internalising, because I'm really not the superhero everyone keeps telling me I am. That's just the me I put on social media. It's not the me who succumbs to a tempting, temporary fade-out and ends up in A&E.

There is a very obvious moral to this story. In fact there are many. 'Just say NO!' being the first and most important. 'Trust your instincts' being the second. 'Marry a man who can get you to your nearest hospital within two minutes if he really has to (and one that knows why you do the stupid things you do, too).'

But even though I just experienced one of the very worst nights of my life – and one I hope my brain synapses fail to memorise because I don't need anymore associative panic attacks, thank you – I'm with Freddie Mercury on this point. He said, 'Being human is a condition that requires a little anaesthesia.' Failed surrogacy, I've now discovered, is a condition where anaesthesia might *seem* appealing, but upon reflection a little Piriton would've done the trick just fine, thanks.

My hangover is a few days of mortifying shame. It's also the lingering feeling of absolute terror, unlike anything I've ever felt before, and that, damn you synapses, I'm already suffering flashbacks from.

It's the next day and Mr B has to go to work on just two hours' sleep. Needless to say, I am planning on cooking the most indulgent, loving meal in my repertoire this evening. Needless to say, there will be no cookies and ice cream on the menu.

I decide to use the day to take the more responsible feel-better action, and that is promoting progress. As penance, I call Jane the coordinator and wail down the phone that this feels worse than cancer. In retrospect, of course it doesn't, but at the time when anyone feels pain on this scale, it's absolutely the worst pain you've ever experienced. I need to get her invested in us so she can prioritise us again. We're not new, shiny international clients anymore, are we? We've been this British thorn in their side for absolutely ages, and we complain about all the mistakes and mishaps out loud. I can't bring myself to kill her with kindness, so I wail down the phone instead. So what now, Jane? Well basically, we start again, again. Only Jane has another sixty clients to look after, plus her own progressing pregnancy, and at this point there are no matches for us on The Agency books.

Until …

A month or so later CEO Zoe calls with a tremor in her voice and a very important question. 'Are you guys religious? No? Oh, that's a shame, we have a wonderful lady who just joined us but she's only interested if you're devout. Are you sure you're not religious? No? Oh, that's a shame.'

And still, there are no matches for us on the books until …

Another two interminably long months of absolutely nothing pass (because when you're in a holding pattern like this, nothing else ever happens. I mean, things happen, sure, but they're never of note), and then:

It's Jane this time. Zoe has dropped off the radar somewhat since the finances phone call. 'Lydia' is a first-time
surrogate, a married mother of three. She's not interested
in our religious stance, but she is very interested in helping us.

So, deep breath. We're ready to jump back in.

You know when you're house-hunting and you're devastated when you lose out on the dream home? The one
you actually end up with is always so much better, right?
So much so that you can't believe you were ever upset
about losing out on that one before. That's Lydia. Lydia
is the dream house. All of the same things have to happen
to get this thing going, but this time we feel different. Our
first Skype call is straight magic. It lasts for two hours
and when we put the proverbial phone down, we're in
tears. She's so lovely. She's so honest and open and
friendly, to the point we feel like we've known each other
forever.

Mr B's very first remark is that Lydia looks a lot like
his little sister and I can totally see the resemblance and
connection there. It's like this was always how it was
meant to be. Her husband Jesse was sat in quiet support
next to her the whole time; it's clear Lydia is the talker.
She's chatty, bubbly and warm. She's, well, she's plain
wonderful. This is it, I can 100 per cent feel it.

And we know exactly what comes next because now,
this ain't our first rodeo. First up, the psychological test
that ensures Lydia will have the required characteristics

and support network to act as a surrogate. Then we do medical clearance, again, and then legal. Ooph, it feels like an even longer slog this time. Like we've just done half the marathon but went slightly off-piste, so we need to go way back to the starting blocks and run it all over again.

But whatever, it's different this time. She'll sail through because it's quite clear she is an actual angel.

So we're not sat in a cloud of anxiety every time an email comes in on 'results' day. We're barely even thinking about it, in fact, until, oh Christ, Dr Hernandez again.

Apparently he has some reservations.

Apparently Lydia's psych test shows 'aggression'.

Oh Christ.

OK, let's think about this a minute, just give me a minute. I mean, who isn't aggressive sometimes, right? I mean, you'd think you could play down aggressive tendencies in a psych test to establish suitability for carrying a baby for someone else so, you know what? I think actually it's *passion*. We met her! She's strong-willed, sure, but that's entirely admirable in my book. She's feisty and sassy and so many more positive things that make her so charming to us. What is wrong with a little aggression anyway? This conclusion is not a deal breaker; it doesn't mean she 'fails' the test, but it has brought up red flags for the ever picky Dr Hernandez. Jeez, this guy is a jobsworth. I am not losing this wonderful woman. Not now. Not after all this time. How is 'aggression' counterproductive to pregnancy? I ask him.

Sure, I can see after Melissa that it's not an ideal outcome, but I'm not sure I wholeheartedly value this psych analysis anyway. Ours was done over Skype with a very bored Spanish lady who wanted to know if either my husband or I had ever been abused by a family member, or suffered a drug overdose. I was already furious that I had to have one of these to determine my suitability to be a parent in the first place. So I'm not bothered. Neither is Mr B. Lydia is however. She's incensed! She's outraged! She's *ever so slightly* combative even, but aggressive? Well, sure, maybe a tiny bit, but she soon calms down when we tell her we won. Dr Hernandez gave us the go-ahead. We're all still in the game.

Funny, hyper Skype calls with Lydia become something we look forward to on a regular basis. It honestly feels like she's part of the family already; we're getting to know her three kids, virtually at least. She calls us 'Mommy's friends from London'. Jesse is definitely a quiet presence in this relationship-building phase, but he works away from home a lot, so we become more of a triumvirate. The big three, willing our way on and talking about the journey in minute detail. It feels great. It feels so different to Melissa.

And then we have a call that dips me in dread a little, and it's so out of the blue I almost think I heard her wrong. It's the very early hours of the morning. Lydia lives in Florida, so again the time difference means we start the calls late, but the nature of our chats mean they go on late too. We're talking about her sisters and how close they all are as a family. 'I mean, we see each other all the time, they're so great, but I'm like the black sheep of the family.' Oh really? We question. 'How come?'

'Because, you know, I have all these tattoos, and I had my kids early, but you know if they tell me not to do something, I just get more determined to do it.' Uh huuuuh, I'm thinking, toes starting to curl a little. 'So how did they take this? You doing this for us?' Mr B asks, interested.

'Oh fuck that, I haven't told them, they'd kill me!'
UM.

This is not the greatest turn of events. I clutch Mr B's hand out of view of the camera while we maintain our rictus grins. One of the prerequisites of The Agency Surrogate criteria is full support from the family. It's actually one of the points in the profile that Lydia will have filled out, and that we read. It specifically asks about her support network and how her family feel about her doing surrogacy. I scroll through my phone and find the profile and, sure enough, there it is, in Lydia's own words:

Are your spouse and other family members aware of your plan to become a surrogate?

Yes. Everyone, including my in-laws, are very supportive.

'So won't your parents tell them though?' Mr B hedges, delicately. 'Oh, I haven't worked up the nerve to tell my parents yet. I have no idea what they'll say.' She laughs.

She laughs! I'm not so amused, but she doesn't seem to think this is a big deal. 'My sisters will say, "You'll never be able to give up a baby in a hundred years," but I'll show them!' If I look sideways, I can see the whites of my husband's eyes as he tries to pretend he didn't hear that. The funny thing is Lydia is sure she's saying something really good and defiant here. I excuse myself to go and throw up a little, and by the time I'm back in the room, I'm as determined as Lydia. Dr Hernandez *cannot* be right about this one; this is OK. It's good in fact. Lydia is as strong-willed as they come, and strong will is such an important value in a surrogate. Family support aside, we're, um, we're sure she's the right person to match with us. Right Mr B? He still looks a little manic, but he agrees with me. This, I reason, is where the US comes up trumps (as it were), and we can thank god Lydia isn't a Brit, because hard as it would be, we know we'd need to shut it down and get out of dodge. In Britain, a surrogate can change her mind about keeping the baby up to six weeks after it is born, no matter that it would genetically be Mr B's child. A comment like this, so early in the relationship, would be a nail in the coffin in terms of worry and trust. It's most likely why The Agency asks if the family is supportive before they sign up any surrogates. Because even though a bulletproof contract would stop her being able to keep the baby in the States, nobody wants that kind of scenario – even that kind of thinking – to crop up later down the line. Being protected by a contract in that kind of event might feel secure, might feel OK enough to move past this brief exchange, but still, it doesn't feel good. We busy ourselves arguing with no one that Lydia would never let that happen, and it's just a quirk she has lied to get on The Agency books. It's typical Lydia, so sassy! It's exactly the kind of thing we love about her and that is how we get to sleep that night.

Needless to say, that conversation doesn't need to come up again, right? I know this is the redeeming thinking of a desperate woman in a desperate situation, but honestly? Apart from that one worrying comment, she seems so wonderful. We can't see aggression in her personality. In fact, Mr B would say he's got where he is today because of his assertive streak (he says assertive, I say aggressive), so really, all of this is far from deal-breaking. And now, poof! It's gone from my mind (ha ha, no it hasn't, but it will do, I'm sure, one day soon).

So we've got this, we've got this, we've got this, we've got an email from Dr Hernandez saying there's something else. Oh good grief, can we catch a break? Please?

11.

What if surrogacy doesn't work?

Because we've done this before we had everything in place to get out of the starting blocks much faster than the last time. And so we're off! We've been off for about two weeks in fact; Lydia has been taking her medication to prep her uterus for the frozen embryo transfer. So, as per the IVF timeline, we're gearing up for the transfer date in roughly a week, depending on the results of this latest scan that will confirm it's all going swimmingly, right Doctor?

Except that's what he's emailing us about. The something else.

Is Mercury in retrograde? I only ask because it's the only logical explanation for perfectly healthy, fertile Lydia to not be responding to the drug protocol. Everyone responds, don't they? I mean I did and I'm basically broken. It's oestrogen that she's taking, which thickens the lining of the uterus to appeal to a passing embryo. Like a beautifully plumped sofa to a very work-weary husband. Ideally, the lining needs to reach between 9 and 11 millimetres for the best chance of successful implantation. Lydia's is only just at 7. It's amazing what years of accumulative bad news does to a person. I have come to expect it as a sure thing when awaiting any results or progress reports, but I spend a lot of time and cognitive therapy telling myself that's not how life works. You see, Sophie? This next result is going to be fine. Great, in fact! Just need a few bits of good news and you'll break the cycle, recalibrate your thinking. Only it isn't. And for the last eight years, sure I've had bits of good, amazing, fantastic news, but the scary stuff has still tended towards 'bad'.

He says we can try a different drug combination, and if she can get up to it, we could risk a transfer at 8 millimetres but it isn't ideal.

'Some people just never get there. It's rare but it happens.'

Oh well, if it's rare then it's bound to happen to us, isn't it. And lest we forget, we only have three precious embryos. Would we risk one on a 'not ideal' situation? Would you? Every delay at this point feels insurmountable, but I know I have to take a deep breath and deal with it. It's what we do.

I have a wonderful friend called Emma who is big in the world of acupuncture. It's how I met her in fact – I was seeing her whilst I had The Russian Experience. My Harley Street doctor sent me there saying 'she makes me better at my job', and so I became her patient, but within only a few sessions it was clear I was meant to become her friend. Maybe it was her own history of breast cancer, maybe it was her love of internet shopping, maybe she twanged some friendship nerve with one of her clever needles, but I remember thinking, 'If I don't get a baby out of this, I'm thankful I get an Emma.' It's true that I didn't get a baby, but she made my reproductive system the healthiest it's been for years: within two appointments I had a period so out of the blue I thought there was something dangerous going on down there, and went to my doctor. 'Oh yes, you're having a period.' A WHAT? (I hadn't menstruated since 2011). 'Have you been to see Emma?' he asked. I nod. So does he. 'You see?'

Nowadays I go round for a cup of tea, and when I've had a bad day at work or a fight with Mr B, she'll stick a needle in my ankle, right there on the sofa, and say 'anger point', in between sips. She's also my fertility counsel, so I seek her advice now. Within half an hour she has the name of someone in Lydia's vicinity who is highly recommended and so (much to Dr Hernandez's disdain), we book in twice-weekly appointments until the next stress-inducing scan.

If I'm totally honest with myself, I still don't know how much I believe in Eastern medicine above Western. It's because there is so much derision among the traditional medical community – Harley Street doctor aside. And when it comes to baby making, there are so many variables, we will never know how effective tiny needles inserted at strategic points in the body were as a contributory factor to success. Unless you send someone with a woefully thin endometrium for regular treatment, perhaps? With tangible measurements either side of the course.

Lydia is nervous, but I tell her how wonderful I've felt during and after every session, and I'm a total needle-phobe. All of which is true. Well, there's not much phobia left in me these days. I've had some serious flooding ther-apy courtesy of cancer and infertility treatment, but if there's one part of the IVF process I'm jealous of missing out on this time, it's the acupuncture. And I'm so pleased when she agrees with me! She comes out of her first session buzzing.

It's lovely, but Mr B is sceptical. Dr Hernandez is strat-ospherically sceptical, he chuckles on the Skype screen when we tell him that's the course we're taking. He shrugs knowingly and says, 'It won't help, but if you want to, sure.'

The downtime between big news appointments or occurrences is quite nice. I appreciate the moments of peace when we have something looming on the horizon but it's not right at my door yet, so I can push it aside and concentrate on watching TV or cooking a meal, like we're two normal people going through life as they'd imagined they might. But just like that, it's at my door again. Lydia's in her scan right now, and I have already started typing an email to our coordinator Jane, ready to instruct her to start all over again, once again.

ARE YOU SITTING DOWN?

Lydia messages us whilst still in the stirrups.

I love a message that tells us it's good news before the actual news comes. And it's better than good, it's perfect.

9.8mm!! I almost jumped out of the chair!!

So, acupuncture, eh? Aside from the proof in the pudding of wonderful news that means we are good to go for the transfer in five days, I am totally taken by the genuine delight in Lydia's tone. It only goes to clarify how unfavourable Melissa's response to me was. How could we have expected that relationship to work out? I was being naive, but it's now so obvious it was naivety based on fundamental desperation. Lydia is practically as excited as we are, she legitimately wants this to go our way, and it fills me with such a warm, delightful hope that I straight up adore the next five days. It's the most exciting count-down yet.

Anyone versed in the intricacies of IVF will know the simultaneous highs and horror of FET day, or ET day, depending on whether your future baby (hope, hope, hope!) needs to be defrosted first, or not. They will understand then, the unique frothing frustration of being expected to go about your normal business at home, while someone else goes to the clinic, gets their sterilised surgical scrubs on, waits for their procedure with a nervous belly and an uncomfortably full bladder. It's so difficult to imagine Lydia just driving to Dr Hernandez's office like it's an ordinary day in Miami, alone. How must she feel? Because how I feel right now is beside the point (I feel sort of horrible and high at the same time, FYI). I'd guess, after the acupuncture angst, that she's kind of anxious. I would hope so, in fact, because that is entirely normal anyway, coupled with the fact she has an extra weight of responsibility on her shoulders. As much as we don't want her to feel that, it's just the truth of surrogacy. Anyone who puts themselves up for this miraculous rollercoaster must be strong enough to bear the burden of somebody else's ultimate dream. Can you imagine? It makes me feel guilty just thinking about it, but again, it's an inescapable aspect of trying to achieve pregnancy for someone who cannot. And it's also the allure, surely. I can fully appreciate the desire to do that for someone else. I know I would not be capable of actually doing it, but I wish I had an opportunity one day to make someone else that happy. Happy isn't even the right word. Complete, maybe? Ultimately content? That's not it either, I'll let you know when I find out what it feels like.

So, first we need to get pregnant. It could be today.

Lydia lets us know when she's in the waiting room and that, yes, she's kind of nervous but mostly super excited. I'm so thrilled that she feels this way, it makes every other part of it all the more wonderful. And agonisingly far away! I know from my own embryo transfers that the whole thing takes a matter of minutes. She will go in and lay down on the standard gynae exam bed, looking anywhere but at the doctor. Actually, she'll probably be looking at the screen next to her that shows them both a hazy grey image of her uterus. The fuller the bladder, the clearer the ultrasound, hence the extra concern of when it's acceptably safe to go to the toilet afterwards without your embryo falling out. It won't by the way, it's like holding a poppy seed in the crook of your elbow while you bounce on a trampoline, but still – every woman worries. He'll then carefully feed a catheter through the cervix, into the middle of the uterus, while he calls the embryologist through with the first of our three embryos nestled in another catheter. This one gets threaded through the first till it's in the exact right spot on the screen, then whoosh! It's flushed out into place, and that's it! Done. Dusted. Pregnant until proven otherwise. Now, go for a wee! OK, wait ten minutes with your feet in the air for good measure, then go.

The first thing Lydia does afterwards is FaceTime us from the bed where she has been instructed to remain, as horizontally as possible, for the next two days. It went well! *Really* well in fact. The doctor was very happy with everything, said our embryo looked absolutely perfect and the procedure couldn't have gone better. So that's it!

There are a couple of schools of thought on the laying down part, but we follow doctor's orders, since that's what got us here in the first place. I can't quite believe we're here, with a potentially pregnant surrogate on a whole other continent. And there's nothing we can do to help. No action I can take to make me feel like I might be giving this new life a better chance of making it. No one can control their own bodies to that extent, but at least when it was me I could feel it, and I could feel like I was trying. One hundred per cent relaxing. Eating pineapple or whatever it is the forums say. Now, I can't do anything except sit here and count my blessings that we've made it this far.

There are no negatives here. It already feels like a miracle and we don't even know if it's worked yet. It won't even know itself – it will spend the next two days trying to embed in the uterine lining, so in seventy-two hours it will either have implanted and we will be pregnant, or it won't, and we won't. I can see absolutely no reason why it won't, so I pretend I don't know myself and I'm going to be optimistic for the next fortnight because, duh duh DUH, we are officially in The Two Week Wait.

The Two Week Wait is a concept that is both loathed and longed for, depending on how far down the IVF path you've been. It is also wrong, literally speaking, since the wait to get an hCG measure (the hormone that the baby produces) that is reliably readable is nine or ten days post-transfer. I guess it's a loose description, technically correct because the agony of waiting spills over two calendar weeks. And it is straight up agony. This will be my sixth. By now, I loathe it and actually love it at the same time, but I don't think it's good for my health.

Love it, because the very act of being within it means we've come this far. We've had a successful transfer, where the embryo made it safely to its new home, rather than being turned away because of a build-up of fluid, say, or having its freezer malfunction and perishing with four thousand of its embryo friends (this actually happened in Cleveland and San Francisco once, on the same day). The transfer is the bit it all builds up to, so once it's done, everything feels very different. The waiting, instead of the doing. Man, that's excruciating.

There is a benefit to it not being me this time, and that is a disconnection to the 'symptoms'. I would feel, and then obsess over, every possible pregnancy symptom, and be *sure* it was happening this time. The cruel truth of the matter is that the progesterone you take during The Two Week Wait mimics the indication of pregnancy. You need it to trick your body into supporting a growing embryo, so the result is sore boobs, a bit of nausea, fatigue et cetera, and it is literally impossible to determine which is real and which is chemically induced. Unless you test early, that is.

The women on all those forums that serve as a highly unreliable *IVF for Dummies* guide, pee on little paper strips every day to check for hormone levels. And you can get those tests that detect an early positive, but they're not as reliable as a blood test, so as hard as it is to pass each of those nine days without caving, it's definitely more sensible, emotionally speaking. Are we going to be sensible? Because good grief I want to know right now! I can't do another day! I can't, I can't, but of course I can. I've done many of them before. I just have to block out all the noise with crap TV or very complicated cooking and try and look forward to results day. There's nothing else for it. We check in on Lydia most evenings and watch her happily chatting, telling us how she's not lifting her kids too much and how much pineapple she's eating. It's quite lovely in lots of ways; it's unusual to be in such a triumvirate during this agonising time and it feels extra supportive, like being in a girl band instead of going out on stage as a solo artist.

And now it's ten days later, no one peed on any sticks in the interim, and I think we all woke up feeling sick this morning (which could be a very good sign for one of us at least).

However, I woke up alone because Mr B is away on business, which is ridiculously bad timing. We tell ourselves it's totally fine because we don't want to put any extra pressure on today. It's just another day! A day like any other, it's totally cool, you go to India, I'll go to work, Lydia goes to her nearest clinic for her Beta test to measure her hCG levels, and then we get the result. The result. I wish so badly that he was here with me because of course it's so far from normal that I can't really manage to eat, let alone work, and I know he'll be the same. Maybe even worse because he's so far from home, and in the event of bad news there will be no one to comfort him, not even the cat.

Anticipation is THE WORST. I hate it, I hate it, I hate it, I hate it. This sixth time experiencing results day is an absolute killer; I think it's accumulative. My own ability to deal with this D-day declined after my first one. When it didn't work, every next chance became more important, each one had the added pressure of diminishing embryo supplies and an increased expectation that it would be bad news, so, all in all, it was just grim. This time is different because it's not me, but I can't help but tie it all up with my previous failures – of course I can't. Today I'm going to be experiencing the same groundhog day of waiting with hope, waiting with sadness, waiting with hope, waiting for the email, refreshing the emails, not wanting to look, wanting to look, and I think that it gets worse every time. This time I thought it might be easier because it's not my body, not my constant mindful symptom-scanning or incessant fear of going to the loo for what I might find in my pants. But waiting on the other side of the world? I think it's worse.

We have only three embryos and, because of our contingency plan being blown out of all proportion, we don't have any more money. We've paid the clinic a package that covers four embryo transfers, so we're OK there. But that doesn't take into account the medication, the local scan appointments, the flying back and forth to Miami, the insurance and the rest of it that adds up to about £7,000 to £9,000 extra per cycle. I know I shouldn't be thinking like this right now, I should be conjuring positivity, sending good vibes across the pond to Lydia's uterus where our baby is about to let us know it exists. Because she had the test four hours ago, so we should be expecting the lab result any moment now.

And so it begins.

I'm refreshing my emails about every two seconds, heart hammering each time and feeling an odd relief when there is nothing new at the top of my inbox.

Mr B, bless him, is having a legitimate conniption over in India, where he waits with me, but miles away from me. He's so anxious that he's been messaging Lydia every hour or so asking if her nausea is still there or if she's extra fatigued. I jump in.

Guys, stop it. We can't guess at this point. We just wait.

Which is EXCRUCIATING.

What I'm trying to push from my mind is the possibility that it hasn't worked, because at this point it will feel like too much of a momentous heartbreak. It will have defied Dr Hernandez's high odds (he gives himself a 60 to 70 per cent success rate), plus there is another person with her own distress or disappointment this time. For that reason, I haven't even told my parents that the transfer went ahead yet, because they're so engaged in this experience that they will have been counting down the days themselves, too. And for that reason, I can't call my mum when I really need to now. Tell her that I'm having a panic attack, feel her comforting presence, because that would take an admission, an explanation.

It's almost the end of the day now and I'm on a train home at rush hour, still refreshing my emails, still nothing. I don't want to receive the news here, good or bad. I'm alone on a train crammed in with strangers. I don't want Mr B to receive it alone on a business trip in India.

Lydia is also waiting, of course, with her kids in America, nervously anticipating the relief that she's done it! Got us all to where we need to be. She tells us that she is so anxious that she can't eat. I feel guilty about the emotional responsibility she must be carrying. It's why I pretend in our chat that I'm not feeling all of these things. Instead I tell both of them that:

If it works, it's super-lucky; if not, we just try again.

Then later:

What will be, will be. There's no point worrying about it because no one could have done anything to affect the outcome.

Then later:

WE'VE GOT THIS!

I don't subscribe to these things, otherwise I'd be eating the dinner that's sitting cold in front of me, rather than chewing the inside of my cheek till it hurts.

Check emails. Nothing.

Check emails. Nothing.

I just sit and stare at the phone, and keep refreshing and refreshing for Four. More. Hours. Until …

It's here! An email from the clinic:

> Hello Sophie. We have the results of Lydia's Beta test and I don't have good news. It came back negative. I'm sorry.

Oh.

I should have known, I tell myself. I shouldn't have hoped. Because I didn't know that I was capable of breaking any more.

12.
How do you keep going?

'I expected it to work. We don't have any reason to think it wouldn't.' This is Dr Hernandez on video call, explaining our failed embryo transfer in a way that I assume is supposed to make us feel better, but actually does the opposite.

The good news he is trying to convey is that we know we have now done everything in our collective power to make this thing work, no suspicions or what-ifs left. We've clarified that we're only using 'perfect' embryos. We've worked out how Lydia best responds to the medication and the transfer went without any hitch whatsoever. The bad news is that there is no reason it didn't happen already, so now we are firmly in the realm of 'unknown'. It feels like falling with nothing left to grab on to. Let's just hope there's a beautifully soft landing at the bottom because as of today, Lydia is gearing us up to start again. We all talked about it together over the last few days and agreed that the only way to feel better is to push forward. As soon as is medically possible in fact, because we've already wasted so much time. Even Lydia feels that way and this is the first embryo transfer she's ever done. There is something about the cyclical nature of assisted conception that makes it feel interminably slow.

Because of Lydia's age and clean bill of medical health, Dr Hernandez sees no reason to wait before trying again, so long as she feels comfortable, too. She absolutely does, with bells on. It's quite difficult to grasp the disappointment a surrogate must feel at a failed transfer. It's interesting to me how the same uncomfortable space between hope and reality can have such different connotations for all involved. For her part, Lydia is more than keen to try again, to achieve what she set out to do, I guess – to help us.

So, here we all go again. Credit card out, medicine ordered and delivered to her at home, brand new treatment plan in place, and there you have it, embryo transfer number two is tentatively scheduled for three weeks from now.

It's also amazing how soothing having a tangible plan really is. I suddenly forget the pain of the failure – of the last six failures in fact. Locking my sights on transfer day and all that will come after it allows me to neatly replace my disappointment with excitable hope. Because that's the exact pull of the fail-repeat cycle, and I'm as susceptible to these particular endorphins as the millions of other women who continue to batter themselves over the head with their own 'next time could be the one' IVF addiction. Exciting, huh? Weirdly enough, it genuinely is.

I can once again go to work with a smile on my face and hope restored in my heart.

As is the nature of an ideal surrogacy relationship such as this one, we check in on Lydia most days and always look forward to the easy chatter. She's settling into our lives in a wonderful way that makes me fantasise about how our baby will see her. She'll be exotic Auntie Lydia who carried you in her belly little one! Look, there's her picture on the wall. We'll go and see her one day when we go to Disneyland and she can carry you from the outside this time! I must say I feel a certain level of healthy detachment that she's all the way in America, too. We were driven to this point precisely because we don't have anyone close who would act as a surrogate for us. But Mr B and I often welcome that fact these days. I wonder how such close relationships pan out once the baby arrives. I bet for every amazing tale of closeness and a unique bond that only strengthens their relationship, there is one fraught with uncomfortable jealousy and misunderstanding. I think this because I've been advised by a few psychologists that there are measures one needs to take to avoid exactly that kind of friction. And they exist because it's really quite common. With Lydia in the States, we don't really need to worry about how I'll feel if my baby prefers a cuddle with Auntie Lydia to one with me, say. I have a colleague whose friend acted as a surrogate for her best friend, and the whole thing sounded absolutely magical in a totally different way. It's encouraging that these stories exist, I love it, but I also love how things are unfolding with Lydia, and so, back to our chat.

She has a sparkle in her eye as she tells us she's going to tell her sisters what she's up to, and she's shitting herself about it, HAHAHA!

I'm not finding it quite as funny. In fact it feels like indigestion as my anxiety resurfaces. Damn it, I thought we'd all subconsciously agreed to bury this topic of conversation. It's great that she wants to come clean, but the timing could be better, Lydia, couldn't it? What if they talk her out of it? What if they disown her? What if we lose our surrogate – because she can pull out of the contract still if she wants to – *and* we're responsible for the breakdown of her family? It's my cue to slope off to the toilet so I can have a silent panic attack, while Mr B carries on the chat. Those two have a unique understanding of each other; it's quite sweet. And quite useful in these scenarios where I feel overwhelmed and he swoops in to rescue me.

When I come back they're on to a different topic and, as is the way with these video calls, by the time it ends we feel so full of love and gratitude that we forget about the faux pas. The mishaps. The silly thing that was, what was it again? So it's all fine!

The next day it's better than fine. Lydia has been for her first scan and guess what? She's responding to the medication perfectly this time. It's brilliant news! It was just an anomaly last time; this is all going to go so exactly to plan that we can fully enjoy Christmas this year with the knowledge that there is probably a baby in some-body's belly!

Christmas represents a terrible time of year for the IVF non-performers. It's a yearly failures benchmark. Oh, here we are again on the day that we want to celebrate with our child, because Christmas is for the children after all, but we don't have one of those yet, so ... This Christmas is a few weeks away and it will be different this time, though. Because this Christmas we will hope-fully be in The Two Week Wait. Only this Christmas the embryology lab in America will be closed for six entire weeks, and no one thought to tell us or factor it into our transfer schedule cycle, so, um, what the fuck Dr Hernandez? What. The. FUCK?!

Even I know that IVF follows a strict timeline, and I know that the medicine that Lydia is responding perfectly to needs to be administered for a certain number of days before the transfer can happen. I know that the embryo needs to be thawed in the embryology lab and placed carefully inside Lydia's uterus on a very specific day, but I did not know the lab would be closed for business. The doctor did, I presume. So why did he make the plan and start the medical protocol when he did? Oops? OOPS?!

He doesn't seem phased. He says we just need to keep her on the treatment plan over Christmas until the lab reopens and then we can reschedule for the New Year. Just like that. Like it's no biggie. But it's a humongous biggie for me. Not only do we have another Christmas dashed, another loathsome delay, but we have to ask this kind woman to take drugs she doesn't strictly need for much longer. And the other thing is that the bloody drugs cost a lot of bloody money. It feels like we are being played with. Like this kind of shift, negligence, is nothing, inconsequential. I would like to punch something. Someone, actually, but instead I put my fist in my mouth and prepare to let Lydia know we need her to keep going a bit longer, for us, please.

Who closes for Christmas for six weeks? What kind of business model is that anyway? Because make no mistake, surrogacy is highly profitable in the US. In fact, the global surrogacy market is expected to yield over $27.5 billion by 2025, largely because of an ever-growing rise in the number of infertility cases. That means many people like me, their reproductive system broken, their Christmases ruined, but at least the assisted conception business is booming! That's probably why the embryologists can afford to sit back and eat turkey for that bloody long. And why we have to swap Christmas shopping for medication shopping, but – deep breaths, deeeeeeep breaths – it's all so that next Christmas we will have another person to shop for. It's worth it, of course it is, it's just endlessly frustrating.

There is absolutely no point asking why Dr Hernandez didn't allow any spare days for contingency when he made this treatment plan, knowing the lab would close the day of the scheduled transfer. I mean, don't get me wrong, we did ask. And we asked again, but we got the most mind-numbingly vague response from his team, there was really no point asking. ('I cannot give you a reason why things were scheduled the way that they were'.) So we keep on keeping on, because that is what we do now. And we drink.

Luckily Lydia is totally fine to stay on the meds. She's willing and cooperative and supportive, but she's also exhausted. Lately she's been grumbling that her husband Jesse has been working away a lot, so she has to look after the three young kids on her own. Oh yeah, Jesse! Almost forgot about him. Since the first video call in fact, because, actually, we haven't seen him since. Hmm, that's a good point Lydia, what about Jesse? Every time I refer to our exciting surrogacy crew, it's always us three. We're a solid transatlantic team, us and her. A soon-to-be triumphant triumvirate. I don't even factor her husband in. And, hmm, now that you mention it Lydia, I'm not sure if that's maybe not so OK. Of *course* she's exhausted, she has three kids under the age of four and a husband who often works out of town for days at a time. She goes to her appointments alone; she flew to Miami for her transfer alone. I never thought about it that much because I'd done it so many times myself. Russia and back. Oh, here we go again, Russia and back. Oh again? OK, I'm off to Russia Mr B, see ya. But that's because I did it so many times it became the norm. Usual. No particular need for a plus one. This is Lydia's first foray into surrogacy, and let's not forget, her family don't know about it still, so where does her support come from? Aside from us of course.

Christmas is inconsequential, insignificant. A typical Christmas of the IVF-er. Nothing much matters apart from that closed fucking laboratory with our embryos imprisoned inside. It's nice, being with my family and eating way too much, don't get me wrong. I love Christmas, obsessed with it in fact, but everything pales into significance to this constant anxiety that hangs a shady veil over everything else in between. At least we have something to look forward to in the post-holiday comedown I guess. The one I usually spend a little bit sad, missing the romantic fairy-light glow and knowing I can't really have an excuse to drink prosecco on a Monday for a while. This time we have a transfer booked in, so while everyone else takes down their trees and leaves them to decompose on an illegal street corner near their house, we gear up for FET day number two. Or seven, since we're counting.

I'm anxious. Lydia is frazzled. Our relationship has become so close that she doesn't mind telling us the ins and outs of her family dramas. It's a conflict of interest that I'm trying to deal with off the record, as it were. As her new friend, I'm all in. I'm so sorry her husband's job takes him away from the four of them, that she is left to look after the small children. I'm a tiny bit thrilled that she's got such big, exciting news to tell her folks this evening, and she's ridiculously nervous but looking forward to it at the same time. But as an intended parent, trusting in her capability to get us to our end goal, I'm anxious. I don't *want* her to be exhausted. Exhaustion is obviously not conducive to IVF success! I don't want the risk of her family's response dropping a bomb in our immediate future. Even if they don't try to talk her out of it, the stress of going against your closest family's wishes is surely not conducive to IVF success. Or anybody's happiness.

So, it's definitely best to get this out of the way now, before we try for the second time. This time is going to be THE time, so we need everything in its rightful place, for Lydia's ducks to be in nice, neat single file, so everything feels as right as it possibly can.

So how did it go? Because I'm over here biting my cuticles to shreds.

'Oh, they were totally cool,' she says, as if nothing just happened, as if my cuticles weren't bleeding. In fact, Lydia's own mum had offered to be a surrogate for her aunt once, donkey's years ago – something that Lydia did know about, so um? So why? So what the ... never mind. It's a brilliant outcome, no matter whether the worry could have been avoided or not. I don't need to worry about what the stress is doing to my body anymore, mine isn't the one we need to take optimal care of right now. And now is the time! Eat those omega-3 fatty acids Lydia, because tomorrow is D-day. Or FET day if we're being more accurate.

It's become like a routine now. Because it's far away, not happening to me, but *for* me, I imagine the transfer process a bit like a movie montage. Lydia boards a plane that touches down in sunny Miami, she hires a car this time, and the next morning wakes up in her immaculate hotel room for the big day, happy and healthy. She messages us from the clinic waiting room, then dons her gown, is shown into the treatment room and waits excitedly for Dr Hernandez. He points out that her lining is perfect, as is the embryo, and guess what? The transfer goes that way too. Cut to me and Mr B waiting anxiously for this recounted news back home. When we receive it we toast her with champagne and shed a little tear of hope, excitement and relief. And that's it! Roll credits. We know what comes next, no need to watch the sequel. The Two Week Wait has started again and this time, it's serious. I mean it's always serious, but this time, it's *extra* serious.

On day one, we were so relieved we still have another nine days to go before the dreaded results day that we were able to enjoy the warm glow of potential pregnancy. On day two it was still there, prominent, glowy. Days three and four were intermediate, kind of fine, OKish. Day five, how's Lydia? Oh she's great, feels sick (googles 'Can morning sickness occur this early in a pregnancy?'), headaches ('Are headaches an early sign of pregnancy'), totally exhausted ('Is it OK to be this exhausted for a successful embryo transfer?'). Days six, seven and eight are best forgotten, the anticipatory dread is building and it's deeply unpleasant already. And then it's day nine and Lydia is on her way to get the blood test – three kids in tow – to set off the first cog in the results day anxiety overload machine, once again.

Don't sleep.

Don't eat.

Eat a bit.

Feel sick.

Refresh emails.

Refresh emails.

Refresh emails.

Feel sick.

Refresh emails.

Refresh, refresh, refresh, REFRESH, REFRESH REFRESH.

Oh. My. God. It's POSITIVE!

Have you stopped breathing? Because I've stopped breathing. Lydia is screaming through the phone, she is beside herself with joy. So is her mum apparently, which is a vast turn-up for the books. Mr B is blind from the tears spilling over his lids, so he can't really read the lab report attached to the email and so, while he and Lydia jump up and down in exultation in their respective parts of the world (not too hard, Lydia), I go over the email with a lump in my throat and a kind of mad swimming behind the eyes.

Sure enough, the email says Lydia's pregnancy test is positive! It's a positive! A BFP, a BIG FAT one as the forums would say. POSITIVE!

Kind of. If you look at the numbers, and understand them as only someone with six previous pregnancy test lab reports under her belt can.

Like, borderline. OK, so basically it's as close to a negative as a positive hCG result can be.

A negative scores between 0 and 5 for the measure of hCG hormone, and a positive is between 5 and 500. Lydia's is 5.9.

I so, so desperately don't want to burst this beautiful bubble we three are experiencing, but in all honesty, I'm out. I've done a French exit – silently left the bubble without letting anyone know. It's just those two left but they don't realise it yet. When I was trying myself, the first time I got a positive the hCG reading was 79 and this was classed as dangerously low by my UK doctor. Sure enough, it had dropped a few days later and I was no longer pregnant. Lydia is at 5.9. There's almost no point considering this good news whatsoever. And yet. And yet, the maddening merry-go-round of IVF addiction tells me miracles do happen. Jane, our coordinator, replies to my private and despairing email to let me know she's had a super-low hCG case before that was a bad reading and went on to become a beautiful baby boy! So you know, there's that.

Mr B is still leaking happy tears all through dinner and so I plaster a fake smile, muster up some enthusiasm and do everything in my power to believe in a bad reading. Or a miracle back-from-the-brink leap in numbers when we do the next test in a few days. I can't fool him though, he knows me too well, so I take the pin and burst his bubble too. It's not going to work babe. This is so low it's basically a negative. Game over. Failure, again.

But he's adamant that it's going to be good news. He doesn't care about numbers. In fact, he tells me, some doctors don't even believe in them! That's how insignificant the hCG score is at this super-early point. He's clinging onto the email from the clinic that said, 'The result is a little lower than we'd like to see, but we remain cautiously optimistic.' Cautiously optimistic. They wouldn't even risk saying that if there wasn't a good chance it will go up by Monday when we have to test again, right? And these are medical professionals, fertility ones no less, so they absolutely know what they're talking about, better than I do, too.

Mr B is a model of cautious optimism. He's thrilled, but he doesn't want to allow the thrill, so he tries and fails to conceal a circumspect up-turn at the corners of his mouth the entire time. Even when he says, 'Why the f*ck couldn't it just be a normal positive result like everyone else's?' Deep authentic furrowed brow, accompanied by an almost imperceptible smile. It's confusing as hell. And he's right. He's defiant that there's a chance. He's right, that right now, for this whole weekend in fact, we are pregnant. Pregnant, until proven otherwise.

Guess how much sleep I got over the next forty-eight hours? None, that's how much. Lydia goes for her repeat Beta blood test on Monday as soon as the clinic opens, bless her.

As far as she is concerned, this is it. She's done it! A pregnancy so positive she told her mum, who is super excited, and now she is eager to make the travel plans for the heartbeat scan in a few weeks. That is the next step once you're over the initial pregnancy test hurdle, to make sure the embryo has a yolk sac and is not just a 'blighted ovum', where the embryo implants but does not develop. Good grief, there are so many scary steps still to overcome.

The timing is not wonderful, since Mr B and I are apart again. Me at a friend's wedding, the fanciest of affairs, but I'm sitting rudely checking my phone under the table at regular intervals. I'm the worst guest, I even snap at someone I don't know who is drunkenly trying to flirt with me. Mr B is at home, knee deep in cold fear, trying to cling onto that cautious vestige of excitement, but so, so over this traumatic anticipation cycle. When will it go our way? Will it be today?

I am sad to say the result is now negative.

The clinic emails the fucking awful, damn expected, so not fair news.

So no, then. Not today folks. And for me, not a surprise, but still. Seriously? I'm beginning to get embarrassed about our bad luck. Among all my worries, I'm worrying about the embarrassment of delivering yet more bad news to my family, who are hoping so desperately along with me. To my friends, who try really hard to keep up with the intricate detail I try not to regale them too much with at dinner parties. Like this is getting a bit boring now. Here comes Negative Nancy and her trail of constant woe-is-me bad news. I think this is partly what spurs me on to immediately straightening my back, blinking away my tears and resolving to make a plan for how to crack on. Because giving up is so not an option right now. Leaving this wedding is though. I sneak out just as everyone hits the dance floor. I need to be at home with my husband, my family – still just him and me, for now. We can't give up, we can't give up. We have one single precious embryo left. Fuck.

Fuck this. I hate this! Surrogacy is supposed to be the last resort in case all else fails. It's expensive and huge and emotional, and I never ever imagined we would be here, already. The last single chance of our last resort. Surrogacy has always been represented as an exotic way to start your family: 'Cameron Diaz welcomed a new baby into her family, via a surrogate', 'Elton John's surrogate is pregnant with twins.' You never hear the agonising IVF backstory that achieves those headlines. So no one really thinks about it going the other way. I never thought about it going the other way. No one really prepares you for that either. Or Lydia I guess. I think she's increasingly frustrated. I even wonder if she's having second thoughts about this whole thing, because our friendly, easy chat has devolved into small talk, which is weird. She's become a bit more elusive with each passing day. I get it, I understand. This is tough on us all, on our relationship, and so I spend my time reassuring her that she mustn't feel bad or a single iota of guilt. That it's not her fault whatsoever and we don't blame her one bit.

She's just so exhausted all the time, she tells us. She knows we don't blame her, she just hasn't got any help at home and it's pissing her off how many appointments she has to go to for this thing that just won't work!

Oh! Well that feels a bit like a punch in the guts. I feel responsible for her, for her comfort. I have a duty of care because of what I am asking her to do for me, but I have to keep reminding myself that she volunteered. And she is being paid a healthy salary too. Oh God. Oh God, oh God, oh God, I hate to say it, but I'm going to say it. I think I do blame her a little bit. Deep down. Or her husband Jesse at least. Why is he leaving her to do all the childcare so that she is so exhausted all the time? Why is that something I worry about every day. This horrible, uncomfortable worry that makes me feel gross, because I'm worrying about someone else's state of mind, and health, for my own selfish reasons. It's times like this that I hate surrogacy. I hate it! Why do I have to sit and bemoan someone feeling this way in case it is the reason for two of my embryos basically dying. I feel disgusting.

There's another thing. A common affliction of millennials everywhere. A propensity to express their emotions or situations through social media. Mr B, Lydia and I connected on Instagram right at the beginning of our relationship, and it's been great. Really lovely to get that insight into someone's life and home and friendships and all the things a photo-sharing app allows. We've never met in real life, but this is a true window into the real Lydia, as ours are to her.

But she keeps putting cryptic posts up, self-affirming quotes, 'I choose happiness over hurt.' 'Funny' memes: 'YOU: You're a fucking psychopath ME: At least I'm on a path babe, sort your life out.' Her captions are getting a little angry. A little, dare I say it, *aggressive*.

I recognise this social media decline. I've seen it before with my friends who are having a hard time with someone or something, and want to express themselves on their public platforms, rather than in real life. Or who are struggling with their mental health and are reaching out for some anonymous support. Or who are going through a breakup. That last one sticks. Is Lydia having some trouble with her husband Jesse? Is that why he's always away? Is that why she's so tired all the time? I take my concerns to Mr B, who is not at all on the same page as me. 'Oh yes, I saw those, sounds like typical girl stuff to me.' It does, to be fair, but that is why I'm experiencing this female intuition, I reason. 'Nah, she's probably had a fight with her sister.'

In fact, that is the more likely explanation. She told us they're a feisty family, that they clash all the time – lets hope this time isn't about her surrogacy situation! I'm being sensationalist, I love a soap opera – I tell myself to step away from the drama and concentrate on the important stuff. Our last chance saloon. The ever-decreasing slump of a mood that, try as I might, I can't help sliding into at this point. One cannot be peppy in the face of failure forever. I am on the verge of doing my own social media cry for help. Instead, I update my regular post for those interested in keeping up with this whole unravelling experience. The interest in my surrogacy story has grown exponentially beyond my friends and family, which is lovely and surprising and, yes, supportive. I guess there's a kind of morbid fascination with the more extreme end of the infertility experience spectrum, which I totally appreciate. I would be super interested if it wasn't me this was happening to.

But it is me, isn't it? And I can't help but feel like it's spiralling totally out of control. What the hell do we do if we have a question mark hanging over Lydia?

13.

What kind of person would offer to be an altruistic surrogate?

My dad knows when something is making me crack just by the way I say 'Hi' when he calls. Even when I muster all the positive tone in me, and lilt a cheery greeting, so he doesn't worry. Like right now. 'HI DAD!' I sing down the phone.

'Oh Sophs,' he says. 'OK, I'm coming to your office and I'm taking you for lunch.'

I don't have the energy to say no, plus this is exactly what I need, and of course he knows it. He's my dad.

Seeing his face, so cheery and out of context in the place I go for fancy work lunches, is enough to make me burst into tears. And so I do. I can't really eat at the moment, so we do more talking and wine drinking instead.

My dad grew up all over the world; his father fled the Russian revolution as a young boy, landing in Turkey where my dad was eventually born, stateless. They moved to Italy, bringing him up in Milan, before finally settling in England. As such, his accent is distinct but indistinguishable, and he has very sweetly grasped a few British phrases and proverbs upside down or inside out. If I tell him I'm tired, he'll say, 'You've been burning the midnight oil at both ends.' Or if someone has done me wrong, then she'll get her up-and-commance. Or whenever I feel bad, be it sick or upset or frustrated or whatever, my dad says, 'I wish I could be inside your body instead of you,' by which he of course means, 'I wish I could trade your pain for mine.' Now, he listens while I frantically worry that we only have one embryo left and I'm having concerns about the emotional and physical state of our current surrogate Lydia, and I wish, how I wish, that we hadn't gone with this agency in America, who keep failing us in so many damaging ways.

My dad looks sad and says he wishes it could be easier, that he could be my surrogate – the sweet, silly sausage – but it does spark a little memory.

Months ago I'd received a really lovely direct message from a stranger on Instagram offering to help if ever we needed it. Since I've been writing about this experience in a national newspaper, more and more people have got to know about my struggles, I've had a steady flow of amazingly supportive messages and, yes, a couple of 'I'd be your surrogate if it doesn't work out' ones. I'm never sure how to answer, but every time I get one it almost makes me teary with gratitude. Surrogacy is such a selfless thing to do here in the UK, where payment is not an option, and therefore not a motivating factor. So the thought of a stranger offering via DM totally blows me away. I want to respond with 'YES PLEASE, RESCUE ME!' but I know that is wholly unrealistic. For one thing, we are waist deep in the American system. It's going to be impossible to extricate ourselves unscathed at this point. Then there are the archaic British laws that chased us out of our country in the first place. But moreover, it's a huge undertaking. An anonymous DM offer to be a surrogate evokes that same feeling you get when someone offers to pay the dinner bill, which makes you automatically refuse. Sort of like that, but times a million. I could never imagine accepting such an offer under these circumstances. I know what a huge decision this is for someone and how it would impact not only them, but their whole family too. So I carefully assume they're probably caught up in my story, wanting to reach out and emotionally driven to help, but not yet sure about what it all entails. Proceed with caution, is my general advice. Know exactly what you're offering, speak to your families about it if you're really serious, think about the emotional impact. And, above all, don't ever feel guilty if you don't think you could do it. (Because I really don't think I could!)

When this message came in we had just done the first transfer with Lydia. We really did need help, but we had no clue what kind or where to find it. I couldn't even comprehend the thought of things not working out with Lydia, we were too far in and we had thrillingly high hopes for round two. But still, I saved it.

And now, nearing the end of my glass, I find this old message and show my dad:

What kind of person would offer to be an altruistic surrogate?

I'm not sure what your exact situation is today … but if you still need a surrogate … I'd love to volunteer (such a weird thing to be messaging!).

I've wanted to be a surrogate for a long time but never got off my arse and done anything about it. I must seem like a weird crazy inst-stalker or something. But I'm not – I'm a normal person, I promise. I have two boys, three and six years old, and I love being a mother (most days) and I would give anything to help someone struggling deeply to be something most of us take for granted.

I am quite a pragmatic person, able to separate my emotions from a situation. I'd want the parents to be totally involved in every step, it would be your baby and my pregnancy.

If this is something you'd at all consider please let me know and we can start a conversation that may help reassure you that despite the shitty UK laws you have options! There's so much more I want to write to convince you this isn't a wind-up, but this message is already too long! If I can ever play a part in your positive outcome it would be my honour.

Now, THAT is how to write a surrogacy approach DM, in case you were wondering.

She followed up to make sure I'd received it a few days later, which definitely highlighted her standout-ness. She certainly seems serious. But still. No, no, *I'm* paying. No really, I insist. OK, let's split it. I replied at the time to say how hard it was to properly express my gratitude for her lovely thought, and that I'm sure it would all work out, but that she was an angel.

But my dad was so touched by her words he couldn't finish reading because the tears were blurring the phone screen. 'For Christ's sake, Sophie, meet the bloody woman! She's an angel!' (I'd already told her that.)

But this is silly, right? We're romanticising over here. I don't know anything about her. She could live in Prague for all I know. She could have changed her mind. She could be pregnant herself, right now. But my dad's not having any of it (he's a romantic), and so, fuelled by heartbreak and red wine, we sit together and compose another message, this many months later.

I replied:

Hi Rebecca,
I don't know where you are in the world, but I'm
wondering if you'd like to meet for a coffee and a chat?
Mr B and I have been thinking a lot about your wonderful
messages and if it still stands, I think it would be nice to
meet. Let me know,
  Soph x

I hate that I'm in this position, I just feel broken, emotionally battered. But as I press send, I feel the twinkle of stranger kindness seeping through the cracks like warm honey. And then I see another message, this time from my husband. Oh yes, husband. Suppose I'd better fill him on our new plans to meet a British stranger from Instagram who has offered to carry our baby. You know, um, make sure he frees up his diary and such like.

My dad went home feeling much better, and yes, I definitely do too, but there's a niggling feeling of, what is it? I can't quite put my finger on it. It almost feels like … like *cheating*. Like we have to be clandestine about it, like I'm doing the dirty on Lydia.

I'm undoubtedly keen to meet with Rebecca, but at the same time I don't *want* to like her. I don't want to feel like she would have been perfect, like she needed to have found us right at the start, before this all went wrong and we got stuck in the States. That kind of regret is going to be difficult to swallow. That presents a very difficult decision and, to be honest, a logistical nightmare.

So what I am even doing then, sitting here in this fancy Japanese bar on a Tuesday evening? I'm nursing a sake, jiggling my leg profusely and waiting for our blind date to turn up. Mr B was right with me on this one; excited to meet Rebecca, so much so that he made a date for the evening after I told him I'd messaged her. But he's apprehensive too, because he knows by now not to get his hopes up, but also, hopes for what? That we love Rebecca and she loves us and it becomes clear that she would be the perfect partner to get us over the finish line, because it won't be as easy as that no matter what the outcome of this evening. Also, we've never met her, she could be anyone. She could be extreme right wing! Although she likely wouldn't be quite so liberal as to endorse surrogacy if that were the case, let alone offer to be a surrogate. I spot a figure making her way across the road – cute yellow leather jacket, unassumingly pretty with a long balayage bob. I don't know how I know it's her, but I just do – maybe we already have a connection! Mr B rolls his eyes at me, but I get up on shaky legs and go to the door to greet Rebecca with my arms wide. I was right! She hugs me back and I stop feeling nervous, just like that.

Damn it, I love her. She's the perfect blind date; funny, sweet, charming. I know within two minutes that I want to make a baby with her, which is basically about as good as a blind date can possibly get, right? How *romantic*. And even better that my husband feels the same way. I'm pretty sure Rebecca does too, because we get on like a house on fire. Of course there is a bit of a job interview vibe thrown in here too, that goes both ways, as we fire questions at each other. What made her think she would be cut out for surrogacy, what our thoughts would be about attending appointments and scans, what does her husband say, where is our doctor based, et cetera ad infinitum. Because there is *so* much to say!

So that's that then, damn it. Rebecca is the kind of woman we dreamt of knowing a couple of years ago before we resorted to America. For all the talk of the law pushing us out of our own country, we had one other huge reason for not doing surrogacy in England, and that is having no one to do it with. Rebecca is the real deal, she is genuinely trying to talk us into how much she would love to help us – as much as we want to be helped it seems. And she's right in front of us! In north London, dammit.

The more we talk to her, the more the benefits of being able to do this in our own country start to crystallise in my head. In fact, the more we talk, the more I realise that all the benefits of going to America that seemed so obvious to us last year have kind of vaporised. I can't even think what they would be right now. All we seem to have achieved over there are repeated knockbacks and struggles, failures and mistakes. A tricky lack of communication and a sickeningly out of control bill. Basically all of the things we were promised wouldn't happen if we 'did it right'.

Rebecca represents a bigger part of me being involved in the experience too. I'd be more of a participant just by virtue of proximity. The more we talk, the more I imagine being present at sonograms, being able to feel her pregnant belly instead of just seeing it via video call. I could feel the baby kick! I wonder if that would make me feel more connected to it before it's even born. Probably. Just being included in this process is something I'd reconciled with myself. It's OK, it's just another loss I need to deal with and this one isn't a biggie. But all of a sudden, presented with the opportunity to actually be involved in a way that an entire ocean kind of gets in the way of, everything feels possible. It feels important.

The one part that really fascinates me about the concept of carrying another woman's baby is the support network. The thought of a husband being so supportive of his wife's desire to become pregnant for another couple, that he actively encourages her to follow her dream. Because it's not just her pregnancy, really. He lives through it with her. It's the best part of an entire year, and since he's seen her in the same physical state with their own children, how that must psychologically impact them as a couple. I think it is nothing short of astounding. Breathtaking that men like that exist. Because, let's be honest, if we're considering biology and evolution and just the mental limitations of 'bloke-dom', this is pretty much teetering on inconceivable – if you'll pardon the pun. But the really crazy thing about Rebecca's husband? She had contacted me on Instagram *before she had even run it past him, that's how supportive she knew he'd be.* 'Oh, he's a mensch. It means basically he's just a really good guy. He'd do anything for anyone.' And he was, fully encouraging her to meet with us as soon as possible, and so here we are.

Wow. Rebecca struck gold with him, I think. Or rather, we struck gold with Rebecca having him!

I think. Because is any of this even remotely plausible? We still don't know if we even need her help, because we have our one embryo over there and one seemingly willing – albeit a bit all over the place – surrogate ready to take us to the finish line. But there are so many buts.

OK so this is where we are:

There is definitely an argument for sticking with what we know. Doing the final transfer with Lydia would certainly be the 'easier' option. Easier! Ha ha, as if that's a thing when it comes to this surrogacy experience. But in this case, although the boat is rocking to the brink of turning over, we know this boat. We have done all the tests and scans and scenarios it's possible to do, so we – and when I say 'we', I mean the medical professionals – literally know Lydia inside and out, as it were. Starting again with someone else would mean going in blind. With one single chance to get it right. In fact, this whole quandary could be totally moot before we've even started because without all the requisite tests, Rebecca doesn't know if she's even medically viable yet.

Also, there's the emotional connection that, try as I might, absolutely cannot be ignored. We trust and care about Lydia. OK, these days I'm struggling a bit on the trust part, because I definitely feel like there is *something* going on. But we absolutely care about her. We've come this far, and by whatever power emotional connection holds, we want it to work with her, even though it now feels like it really might not. Are we mad? To keep doing the same exact thing and hoping for a different outcome? But this is the thing about IVF, with its millions of variables: it could be just one simple decision that is the difference between winning or losing. I mean, what if third time lucky is a thing? What if affection or emotional connection is the feeling that last embryo is looking for when it decides whether to settle in or not?

The morning after our amazing meeting with Rebecca, I wake up with a little clarity. We will let biology decide.

I call my favourite fertility doctor, Mr Hiyer. He's the one who has helped me so kindly and gently since this all started. We book an appointment for Rebecca to go and see him to work out whether we even have a decision on best next steps to make. And then we think about talking to Lydia.

Only I don't want to. I'm too nervous. I don't want to freak her out or let her down or, or … And then I mentally slap myself around the face.

Surely Lydia ultimately wants the best chance of success for us. Surely her motivating force was altruistic: helping a recurrently unfortunate couple of strangers have a baby. Even though, yes, money would be involved, which may or may not be the overriding motivator, I refuse to believe she isn't thinking of us with compassion and empathy first and foremost. We know her! If we're not getting positive results, for whatever reason, and we have one precious embryo left, she would absolutely want us to work out what gives us the best chance, and then take it, right? Right? That question is going to have to wait because I can't do it. I'm too afraid of hurting her feelings to ask her thoughts about moving forward with someone else. So, what I'm really saying is, I'm risking our future happiness out of politeness. Yup. I'm a pathetic mess.

And then, as if I'd summoned it into being just by thinking of Lydia, my phone pings a message alert.

So does Mr B's. He comes into the room holding his phone out at me, looking worried.

What kind of person would offer to be an altruistic surrogate?

It's Lydia.

Guys, we need to talk.

Please let this be the first time in the history of that foreboding sentence that something positive follows.

14.

How do you deal with the international divide?

We have to wait until Lydia is ready to FaceTime with us, when she has finished work, done dinner, put the kids to bed and taken the time difference into account. This means a whole day of work, biting our nails to knuckles and passing on dinner, until we find ourselves in bed at one in the morning, waiting for her face to appear on Mr B's laptop screen. 'We need to talk' is a term that has no right existing in the British language. It is ominous AF. This is like being told your boyfriend is going to dump you after school, then having to endure an entire day of lessons before having the heartbreaking conversation in person.

I'm ridiculously anxious, which is helping me battle the tiredness of being awake at this unearthly hour, even though I have an inkling of what is about to unfold. Despite us having such a lovely time with Rebecca, how I feel right now is telling me I don't want to drop a bomb in our situation. I don't want it to become precarious all over again, to experience all the unknowns we spent the last year or so overcoming. So now, as I wait with my heart in my mouth, I'm hoping I'm wrong and this call is not about to throw a spanner in the works because, really, we have an abundance of those already. Mr B is quite calm actually, reassuring me that it's probably just a friend spat, girls will be girls, social media is not an accurate representation of what's going on in real life. He's right on all counts, but still …

When she does come on the screen Lydia is fidgety and small-talky and it is ridiculously awkward. I can't hold my wobbly fixed smile for much longer, so finally it's me that drags the elephant into the middle of the room. I say, 'What is it you need to talk to us about?'

She looks sheepish, squirms a bit with an 'oops, you caught me' expression, and then …

'So, um, I'm getting a divorce.'

Audible gulp from Mr B. Hide the panic, hide the panic. I *knew* it! Well, OK, this is actually worse than I'd been fearing. '*Getting* a divorce' suggests the relationship has been breaking down for a while now. No one gets a divorce the day after a happy marriage, do they? It's not an impulsive kind of scenario as far as I know. But no, they have the papers all drawn up already. My limited experience of lawyers (house-buying) tells me that the entire process must have been somewhat drawn out, so, um, what the hell? And on top of the worry for us, and the yes, genuine dismay for how awful this must have been for her, I feel a real conflicted dismay that we weren't privy to any of it. I mean, is it even OK for me to feel that way? It's her life, her marriage, her business. But such is the nature of a surrogacy arrangement, when it comes to her life right now, it is inextricably intertwined with ours in a way that blurs all sorts of boundaries. I'm asking her if she is OK right now, but what I really want – no, need – to know is, has she *been* OK this whole time?

We listen as she tells us she is in fact more than alright, this is the best thing. Actually, he wants to try again but the marriage is already dead to her. Oh my goodness, my mind is reeling at the same time. I can't help feel a creeping sense of unease that we might even have contributed to this sad outcome. Was it the strain of surrogacy? Are we in some part responsible for the break-up of a marriage? I can't even begin to— Hang on a second, though. I need to think, and it's very difficult with all the chatter and the early hour and the super-bright screen. But the basic facts are there and they won't change. They *both* signed up for this when they did, knowing the strength of their relationship at that time. The initial screenings and the psychological evaluation are to protect both the surrogate and the intended parents. They are to put everything in the right place for a great experience and best outcome possible. Yep! All the imperative steps in the beginning were to make sure this exact kind of thing wasn't happening. Or at all likely to happen. So then, what the hell happened?

That is a question to be processed at another time, though, because facts and what-ifs aside, we're faced with a girl – a new friend – who is telling us something huge and hugely personal. And so, naturally, we offer our wholehearted support. By now we've built up a rapport where she clearly sees Mr B as a kind of big brother figure, and me as a woman who went through some shit, but has her shit together, and as such she sort of looks up to us. And so as such, she's worried we'll judge her. As it happens, judgement is the last thing from either of our minds. For one, I suspected there was trouble in paradise, and for another, this is sadly one of the more common pieces of news being delivered in my social circle. Of the many friends' weddings I've been to since Mr B and I got married eight years ago, about half have already split up. It's a sad societal condition, but it's certainly not unusual. There are always valid reasons for the breakdown of a marriage and Lydia's and Jesse's shouldn't matter to us. Unless, of course, it *is* us.

Is it us? She's fundamentally reassuring without me having to be quite so solipsistic as to ask, telling us he works away so much that she has basically been a single mom to her three children the past six months or so. And so yes, she's exhausted.

And so here we are. The deeply murky waters of international commercial surrogacy that The Agency screening process is there to save us from. When we first match and meet and plan, we have to trust that our surrogate is happy and healthy, open and honest, and wouldn't keep a critical change in circumstances from us. There is even a clause right there in the contract: 'must declare any change in circumstances immediately'. But then, I guess, that's also where it's quite murky. It's a vague clause, really quite grey. Why would she tell us if she's just at the 'having issues' stage? When does it go from 'having issues' to 'change in circumstance'? Emotionally, I understand why she waited until crunch time, until the divorce was definitely happening, but if she were being taken on as a potential surrogate by a doctor or agency in the US and she declared a relationship breakdown, she would be rejected. There is a reason for that: it's to do with protecting her mental and physical health, optimising success rates, minimising potential disruption and mutual stress – all the obvious cons that make divorce incompatible with surrogacy. So, at this point down the line, what is the difference? She said she's been having issues for six months or so. That is before we even met her and Jesse. Woah.

Clearly there is a conflict here that goes beyond Lydia's marriage issues. Could this obvious stress and exhaustion be the reason our first two embryo transfers failed? And even worse, I actually feel selfish for having these thoughts, when the impact on our journey seems the farthest worry from Lydia's mind right now.

Lydia keeps inadvertently dropping bombs, telling us The Agency knew – they KNEW! – and advised her to share the news in her own time, when she was ready. Now, this is absolutely true and sound relationship advice. When it comes from a friend who is counselling you on sharing the sad news of your marriage breakdown with the rest of your friends. It is absolutely not true and sound advice when it comes to a commercial surrogacy agreement, where fundamental criteria are out the window. It is definitely not in the best interests of The Agency's fraught international surrogacy clients, who potentially just discovered why two of their precious three embryos didn't implant.

Argh! This is all starting to feel seriously out of control and only getting worse. It's where the murky waters of commercial surrogacy become a whirlpool and I can totally feel myself being sucked under. Guessing and culpability and correct processes and contract breaching and relationship straining and duty of care and really, I have to admit it to myself now, *serious* mismanagement from an agency that keeps letting us down. This is where America falls down. There is no precedence for this, so we have a disturbing task ahead of us to work out exactly where this emotional bend in the road leaves us, logistically, economically and bureaucratically.

Ultimately, this is where I'm getting lost. Where does emotion end and business begin? Is it starting all over again? Is it picking up broken sticks and giving up on America all together? But at this point, we've spent in excess of £150,000 on making it work there, money we don't technically have. So we can't just walk away. Can we?

I'm not sure when this all became so emotionally entangled, but I don't like it. First, I'm trying not to perceive the entrance of this new potential surrogate into a weird kind of infidelity triangle, and now we have a divorce thrown into this morally delicate hot pot. I hate the uncomfortable turn this is taking, and I don't understand why it's even happening at all when we specifically went to America to enlist an agency who was supposed to mitigate this kind of situation for us.

So there we have it, I guess. We now have this horrible aggravating factor that might be the reason it hasn't been working with Lydia so far. In fact, Dr Hernandez's advice after the last failure – even without knowing about this divorce – was to consider investigating other options for our last chance. It felt impossible at the time. It felt uncomfortable but almost fathomable when Rebecca came onto the scene. And now? Well now, as sad and outrageously unfair as it feels, it's abundantly clear that we need to call it a day with Lydia, isn't it? We can't go forward in good faith knowing what we know. So, in essence we're also going to have to dissolve our relationship with her. Poor Lydia. Two divorces in one week.

We're going to give the news to The Agency (stupid, incompetent agency) and Dr Hernandez first. Give me strength.

Our conversation with Jane at The Agency is brief and to the point. Worse than that, I can't bring myself to talk to her anymore, so Mr B sends an email, something to the effect of 'How could you know this vital information and think it best not to tell us? At what point does this become a contract breach? How did we manage to trip and fall into your hands, of all the bloody surrogacy agencies in the United States?' That last one wasn't included, of course. And we already know the answer to that – whoops, my fault. Nothing more than due diligence gone wrong. But I still maintain, with something as uncommon as surrogacy, you don't know until you know. That's my story and I'm sticking to it. And this is where the issue lies. She wasn't apologetic, she didn't worry about any contract breach because there was nothing that stipulates, 'In the event of the D-word, all parties must be told immediately.' Rather, she said it was Lydia's news to tell. And this is the reason I cannot deal with her, anymore. I just cannot. Jane is part of the reason I am bolstered to close the door on Lydia, because every interaction at this point fills me with white hot rage.

But not with Lydia, that part is way more delicate. We tell Jane that we're looking to pursue a surrogacy arrangement with someone else, over in England. No agent needed in the end, thanks. And then Mr B asks Jane to respect our wishes to let Lydia know ourselves, telling her, 'We will likely have a continuing relationship with Lydia, so it's important to us that her wellbeing is considered at all times now and once told this project is over.'

The thing is, I really hope a relationship with her is even possible once this is over, because she's becoming more and more despondent and yes, aggressive, with every new interaction. Because, hmm, how to tell someone we don't want to continue our surrogacy journey with them because of their divorce without making them feel judged? Or not worthy, at a time they're likely feeling quite crap already. And then I keep having to remind myself, we are also feeling way worse than crap. Have been for a good few years in fact. This is a horrible situation for all concerned and, if it works out with Rebecca (the other woman as far as Lydia is concerned), we have decided to manage the explanation slowly over the next few months as we establish this new journey. Is this OK? We want to let her down gently, so we are delivering bits of news at a time. For starters, we had a frank conversation with her yesterday to explain we need to put things on hold for a bit because we have run out of money. This is 100 per cent truth, and it's terrible because it means even if we decided to pursue our last chance with Lydia, we would be in serious financial dire straits. I discovered this when I spoke to my wonderful London doctor Mr Hiyer. We had a long chat, where I explained to him what was going wrong (hence the length of the phone call) and what our options might be if he screens Rebecca and she is deemed a good candidate for surrogacy, physically speaking. Mr Hiyer works with several international fertility clinics where he sends his patients for donor egg treatment, so he has some strong knowledge of the surrogacy process in the States, and he was pretty appalled by my recounting of our story so far. His colleagues in Washington were also appalled. He reported back that it was worrying we had spent so much money to get to this point. And worse: 'The biggest spend happens once the surrogate gets pregnant. That's where the bulk of the payment comes in. With the fee and the hospital and medical costs, you're looking at around £70k best-case scenario.'

Fuck. We don't have £70,000. We don't have £5,000 at this point. It's like a renovation project that we undertook without a survey; everything has gone on mending the cracks so far.

I don't know why this is such a shock to me, but it's frightening how we got to this point. One wrong turn at the beginning and we somehow got lost in the maze.

More misalignment from The Agency it seems. More news we weren't prepared for this far down the line has become par for the course in our case, but it only served to solidify our stance at this point. We wouldn't be able to make it work with Lydia even without the divorce. Not right now, anyway. And it seems infinitely kinder to let her know this is the primary reason for terminating our journey with her, rather than letting her know she was usurped by another woman. As totally crazy as that sounds, this is what our experience has taught us. Emotions are high, Lydia is sensitive. Knowing her, we assume hearing about Rebecca right now would make her feel worse, and we don't want to risk that.

So yes, we told her we would need to look for a more cost-effective solution to our mounting surrogacy problem, so she is aware that we are not giving up completely. In case she stumbles across some wonderful social media post in nine or ten months (please, please, please let it be) and feels shocked, angered, put out, lied to, anything negative at all. Because right now she does *seem* to be feeling quite negative. She nods understandingly over our video call, but she chews the inside of her lip in a questioning way at the same time. Could she actually be taking it as a personal slight? Is that even a possibility? Because she's saying the right things, well, OK not saying very many things, but her demeanour seems, I dunno, pissy? All I can think of is to send more and more supportive messages and concentrate on getting to a place where we even have a reason to let her down gently. Rebecca and I have our appointment with Mr Hiyer tomorrow, and then we'll know one way or another.

I'm decidedly nervous. Lydia was our fourth surrogate, found through a professional agency. This suggests to me that there are so many factors and criteria and reasons why so many women aren't 'good candidates', so what makes us naively think Rebecca will be? I'm quite sure we can't be that lucky straight off the bat. A stranger wanders into our lives, in the role of superhero sent to save us, and is perfectly qualified for the job? Nah, this is us we're talking about. So yes, I feel sick while we wait together in the reception of his beautiful clinic. It's also quite odd to be here with her, only our second meeting in real life, and this one is not quite as pleasant for her as a cocktail in a sake bar. I almost wish I wasn't here actually, it wouldn't feel so corporeal. Asking someone to take the role of my womb – presenting them for medical inspection – well, it does feel as gross as it sounds, to be honest. This is an unquestionably odd situation, and the moral connotations are impossible to ignore at certain points in the journey. This is definitely one of them. But I look at Rebecca and she is positively fizzing with excitement. She's just a delight to be around, not least in this waiting room, waiting to find out if she is able to do this thing she so badly wants to do. And OK, when you put it like that, my misanthropic perspective is totally blown out the water. Such is the crazy nature of surrogacy, of altruistic surrogacy, specifically, which is absolutely growing on me the deeper I get into it.

There's no need to go into the ins and outs of a medical viability screening; it's as you would expect. Intimate, not uncomfortable, but definitely private. So once I'd sat and had a lovely chat with Mr Hiyer and Rebecca, I was ushered out of the room while he worked out how likely to achieve a donor egg pregnancy she would be. 'Perfect!' he tells her. 'Perfect!' she beams at me, when I go back in. 'Perfect?' I ask, incredulous. Right first time, Rebecca *is* a qualified surrogacy superhero. So it looks like this is really happening. Now I just need to talk to Dr Hernandez about our last transfer being with a different surrogate, and working internationally along with Mr Hiyer to sync everything up and, who knows? The Two Week Wait could be on all of our horizons very soon. I feel sick, but at this point it's impossible to determine what part of the hysteria spectrum is the contributing factor. We make a date to speak with Dr Hernandez as soon as possible. Or at least we try to; this is the most unresponsive clinic in the world, remember. So we make a date. I said, we make a date. Hellooo? Anyone there? Can we please make a

225

date? Give us a date, WE NEED A FUCKING DATE. And so, we got one, eventually.

So, next stop on the Make Surrogacy Great Again rollercoaster: Dr Hernandez, Please Help.

Dr Hernandez isn't that keen on helping. Initially he said he doesn't work in tandem with other doctors like this. He says, 'I need everything controlled in my clinic ... But I think I can do it for you. I think you've suffered enough.' Then he said he wanted to Skype her first to sort of medically interview her for the role, while he and his team spoke about the logistics of transferring our last embryo into a British surrogate with all of the medical prep for the transfer cycle done in the UK with Mr Hiyer.

He advised us that using a new person for our final embryo transfer would have the same chances of success as using Lydia (remember, that was before we told him about the divorce). In fact, he was concerned as to why it hadn't worked so far with Lydia and suspected it was *best* to move on, so it all seems good, right? We're on the right path, we're getting our ducks in a— Oh. Somewhat confused then about this email I just got from him. Floored, actually.

> I have decided that we will not do an embryo transfer into a surrogate from the UK where surrogacy is not even considered. Therefore I see no reason to talk to the potential candidate over a Skype.

What? This must be a mistake. A simple misunderstanding. I suspect it's a side effect of having no international consensus on surrogacy. The rules and regulations of commercial surrogacy in the States are incompatible with those of altruistic surrogacy in the UK, and I get that. It's why I was initially somewhat opposed to doing it in England in the first place. My how things have changed by this point. I just need to explain to him that yes, there is no *commercial* surrogacy in the UK, therefore we cannot pay the surrogate or sign an ironclad contract. But it is, however, perfectly legal to transfer an embryo into our UK surrogate. We checked. In fact, women travel from the UK all the time to do IVF or surrogacy in the US. It seems to me that he is just misinformed and really quite bullish, actually.

I have also already paid Dr Hernandez for this transfer as part of a package, remember, so if he is saying no because of a misunderstanding in international surrogacy laws, then he is sitting on about £15,000 (I know) for the last procedure that he is choosing not to do. Knowing our circumstances, and not budging. He *must* be smarter than this, he is a doctor for goodness' sake.

Come on now, surely it isn't possible to work in an industry as caring and delicate as fertility medicine if you don't care. So I appeal to him. I start with a heartfelt email in response. I tell him about Lydia's divorce and the worry of whether she is emotionally able to continue. I explain about the £70,000 difference between proceeding with her in the States versus an altruistic NHS pregnancy in the UK. We reassure him of the legal stipulation in the UK, of Rebecca's altruistic motivation. She and her husband even write him the most outrageously beautiful letter of intent, and then we put him in touch with wonderful Mr Hiyer, to speak medical professional to medical professional. Mr Hiyer sent me the correspondence and it was perfect. He personally explained his credentials, that he has worked on many international surrogacy cases and therefore can absolutely assure him it is actually 'considered' and also entirely legal in our country.

All this effort and love and support from every angle is so heartwarming that despite this escalating situation that necessitates it, I suddenly feel so lucky. What an absolute dream team. He only needs to read the first two lines of Rebecca's letter and he will relent, no doubt. It's our last hope, after all. It's our precious embryo, chilling over there in his embryo refrigerator or whatever, until Rebecca can be the one to bring it home. Please bring it home.

And so, at last, he replies to Mr Hiyer, cc'ing in Mr B and myself:

It is a pleasure to be in contact with you Mr Hiyer.

Good start. Mutual respect, he'll listen to reason.

Unfortunately, as you were informed in a recent email I sent to Sophie and her husband, I will not help them with

> their request to do an embryo transfer into a British
> surrogate.

I'd also appealed to his kind nature (!) and asked him to
consider refunding us the £15,000 for the pre-paid procedure he wouldn't be doing. It's chump change to him,
surely, relative to how much they charge for us international patients. And now it is quite literally going to be
money for nothing.

> In reference to your request for a reimbursement, after
> reviewing it with all parties involved, I regret to inform you
> that we are not able to honour it.

Ooph. Full-force transatlantic gut-punch. Fuck.

FUCK. FUUUUUUUCK. There is absolutely nothing I
can do about this. It is insane to me. Unfair, I'm incredulous, I'm helpless. I'm bashing the keyboard of my laptop
in frustration and probably causing further water damage
from this incessant damn crying.

But there's another heroic soul in the cc field, and he is
determined to help, so fires a response just in time to save
my heart from total aortic collapse.

Mr Hiyer has a plan.

15.

How many people does it take to make a surrogate baby?

We need a new doctor. Stat. Because, dammit, we are still tied to the States in one fundamental way. Our embryo lives there, and it's impossible to bring it home. It's those blinking international laws again. According to UK law, you can only pay an egg donor up to £750. We used an egg donor in America and we paid her an extra zero on the end. Actually, somewhere north of that. Even if we could gloss over that part, there's the issue of anonymity whereby our anonymous US donor would need to agree to waive her request to remain anonymous and have her details added to a UK donor database. Likely? Ha ha. So OK, Rebecca and I need to go over for the transfer. OK, so we need a new doctor.

And Mr Hiyer has a plan. His solution is genius. No one is stopping us from sending that embryo to another part of America. He and his colleague counterpart at this amazing and revered fertility clinic in Washington could plan our great escape. The idea is to rescue our little last chance from Dr Hernandez and send it to Dr Strauss' lab. We would do the IVF cycle at home with Mr Hiyer, then

Rebecca and I would fly to Washington for transfer day. When a positive pregnancy is achieved (wish pray, wish pray), she'll be back home in England, where I can be alongside her growing belly, rather an ocean away. It's simple. It solves everything. I wish I had known of Dr Strauss and his wonderful clinic coordinator Annabel in the first place, because just one day later we get a call from him. The long and short of it is he wouldn't normally accept embryos from another state, but this time he will make an exception because he's spoken at length to Mr Hiyer and he's horrified by our treatment thus far. The relief is absolutely incredible. It actually makes me shiver all over and my legs feel wobbly all of a sudden. It's like we are slowly edging towards the right set of variables to make this baby happen and it's quite hard to believe. I don't trust myself to take a breath yet, it's too soon to feel happy.

Also, Lydia is cross. She's angry in fact. I suspect there were too many cooks involved in managing this situation delicately and now the broth is totally spoilt and she's texting us some upsetting messages:

> It was brought to my attention that Dr Hernandez is now aware of me wanting to get divorced which is now part of the reason I can no longer proceed in this process.
> Explain this to me.

Oh.

Wow. A totally out-of-the-blue complete one-eighty. I'm so shocked at this somewhat aggressive stance. I totally appreciate this once wonderful plan of action is crumbling around us all, and she must be feeling some guilt because that sadly is difficult to escape when your body won't cooperate with what you need it to do. I should know, I can relate. But there are a few things at play here. Firstly, it seems that she is aiming to continue as a surrogate and complete a family for somebody else. That is fine, of course. It's great, in fact, more lives created and saved all at once. She did tell us she wouldn't be doing it for anyone else, though. That she loved our profile and ours alone, so whilst it's entirely her prerogative to change her mind, how were we supposed to know? At the same time, if I thought another couple were about to embark on a journey as fraught as ours because of the difficult emotional scenario involved, I still would have preferred they and their doctor knew what they were dealing with. But the kicker here is the dismay of her misunderstanding the situation. It seems she is making our metaphorical break-up about her ability to continue as a surrogate, rather than our ability to be parents to this last embryo.

This is one letdown too many for Mr B. He's heartbroken, I think. We've all built a relationship, but they had a particularly poignant connection whereby Lydia felt a bit like a little sister. He can't deal with the sudden about-turn, on top of everything else we've got going on, and so he kind of shuts down to her. I guess it's up to me to try to placate her, because after the debacle with our last surrogate Melissa, the last thing we want is another antagonistic exit. Especially not with Lydia. I try to explain reasonably that of course we have to take our last chance, and then give it the best chance possible. I explain that everyone is a bit emotional, which is to be expected. That we are devastated that this didn't work out with her because we love her!

She comes back with this:

> It took me a while to respond because I'm shocked and confused. Can you please explain to me why the clinic says you are talking to a British woman and they 'understand why you don't want to continue with Lydia'.

OK, this is getting ridiculous now. Can we explain? We've been explaining for the past year. Starting with every word she read of our profile when she chose to help us. We've been explaining during every 1 a.m. Skype chat, where we tried not to express our sadness, instead focusing on encouraging our wonder team forward. In every WhatsApp message we've exchanged, hopes we've had together, results we've received. Were we not in this together? Because otherwise, why is she so cross?

It is becoming glaringly obvious why there are such divided schools of thought on altruism versus commercialism when it comes to UK surrogacy laws versus US. How can you ever make sure that the motivation of a person is true and clear when a significant amount of money is on the table? How can you avoid this kind of fundamental misunderstanding, based on common goals, when the goals might be very different? Umm ... probably by taking the money out of the equation.

I just wish the rest of the UK's parental order laws could keep up with this rational way of thinking, because the original fears about doing it back home still stand. We're still stuck between a rock and a contractless hard place, where should Rebecca fall pregnant, she could change her mind up to six weeks after the birth and decide to keep the baby.

We need implicit trust. We thought we had it with Lydia, but I guess she was presenting the best version of herself right at the beginning, much as you would any other job interview, I suppose. We were effectively employing her, after all. Man, I'm dismayed that we got this all so, so wrong right at the start. I'm dismayed that we didn't have any other choice.

It doesn't feel right to 'explain ourselves' to Lydia via our usual method of swapping short text messages, so I want to send her a considered last goodbye. I want to calm down and think about what she needs from our last exchange, rather than what I need to say. Because we have a plan to continue on our Mother Project, thank goodness. We don't need to leave broken hearts in our wake.

Dear Lydia

Sorry it has taken me a few days to get back to you, but I wanted to collect my thoughts before responding.

I can see why you might feel confused by the way this has shut down after a whole year of us all trying to get to this amazing goal we set out to achieve, but please try not to take this personally. This is exactly why surrogacy is such a delicate issue and it's really not easy for anyone involved, because we each have our personal stance, goal and motivation. We are each the centre of our own journey, and I get how every decision can be amplified or even misunderstood.

Lydia, I hope you realise that there is a medical reason why the doctors and also the surrogacy agencies deem it policy to reject surrogates in the midst of a relationship breakdown. Whether or not you feel strong and capable is not even relevant to the professionals who have a wider criteria, that unfortunately you do not fulfil.

I understand you are cross that we informed the doctor of your change in circumstance, as this now halts your chances of continuing as a surrogate with this clinic for now. But what would you have told the psychologist at the start of the next opportunity with another couple? What would you have told Dr Hernandez if he asked you? The truth, I hope.

Lydia, I just want you to understand that if you are suggesting the troubles you have had with Jesse were something to hide, then by your own admission that would be an issue for surrogacy. Our goal is a successful surrogacy – nothing else – so naturally we want all the facts presented to the medics. Whether or not that affects your suitability, or our chances of success, is not for us to determine. We leave these decisions to the medical professionals.

We have one embryo left and we are blessed that a British surrogate has volunteered to help us. You might ask yourself why would we transfer it to a UK surrogate and not Lydia, right? It sounds awful to say to you, but we cannot afford to continue to do this in the States. There have been so many obstacles and mistakes, and the bills have become scarier and scarier. It's way beyond what we were ever told by our agency, ever expected or ever planned for. We have been offered a lifeline from a UK surrogate who will not charge us any compensation because that is the law in England. There will be no medical bills or insurance etc because we have the National Health Service, which means medical services provided by the government (kinda like what Obama tried to do with Obamacare). If we were to continue with you, it would cost us another $70,000 that we just don't have. If you look at this simple math, combined with the professional advice, I hope you would make the same decision.

That embryo is our future; it is our choice and it is potentially our baby. You would do whatever it takes for your babies. This is nothing personal against you.

I'm going to close with saying thank you for everything from the beginning of an adventure that sadly didn't work out. We will always remember and focus on the good times we all had.

Please take care, be happy, and we wish you a wonderful life with your beautiful family, Sophie and Mr B x

Sadly, our explanation didn't elicit a response from Lydia, but I think everything that surprises or confounds me at this point is just part of the weird and wonderful education of international surrogacy. I'm sure I've learnt something from this, but I'm not quite clear on what it is yet.

So I guess that's it then. The door firmly closed on this particular American surrogacy saga. Goodbye to Lydia, to Dr Hernandez and to our Agency coordinator Jane. And goodbye to an eye-watering, life-limiting amount of money and two years of our lives.

I have to look at it like we're moving home. America was definitely the wrong house, it was erected on a decidedly dodgy foundation, but this next one is so much better. And we've almost, almost got the keys in our hands. So this was all meant to happen because now we have a whole new place to settle into, and this one lets more light in.

As with any medical experience I've had thus far – and I've had way more than I should have – I'm learning to trust in only a few. It is totally OK to move on from people or doctors who aren't helping you as they should. And although it's been a shockingly difficult education, it's an important one. Doctors don't necessarily tick all your boxes but they might tick someone else's, so let them go and tick along elsewhere, rather than bash your head against a clinically shiny vinyl wall. The thing with surrogacy is that there are high emotions at stake; a lot of other people's sensitivities to consider and/or contend with, and that includes the professionals, by the way. The fuckery of surrogacy is that you have to keep *everyone* happy, if at all possible. But somehow we've collected some disappointing detritus in our wake. By now we have been stranded by a Russian doctor, who unceremoniously dumped us because she didn't like the tone of an email. We have been desperately clinging onto a journey with a surrogate, whose feelings we didn't want to hurt even though the warning signs were all there, all along. We've been paying a useless agency for a job that we have been doing 90 per cent of, and we've been stuck with an American doctor who seems to hold all the aces. And all of this has accumulated because we don't want to rock the boat. Imagine gambling your life on making sure the waters are still at all times. Man that's exhausting. And frustrating. And fucking unfair.

So when you find good people, you hang onto them. It takes way more than two to tango when it comes to this particular route to parenthood. By now I've pretty much accrued a bona fide entourage. My crew of angelic experts who will always be baked into my future baby's history, because we couldn't keep it simple like most parents, could we? Nah. At this point I wouldn't have it any other way. So how many people does it take to make our baby?

Mr Hiyer

A great example of a very, very good guy. Because he's a gynaecologist who, by some miracle, made me feel comfortable, mentally and physically, when it was my turn in the stirrups. But more than that, he has always gone above and beyond for us. This is where the care part of the doctors code comes in and, believe me, not all of them are equipped with it. Mentioning no names *coughs* Dr Hernandez, *coughs again* Dr Sokolov. I could keep on coughing but I don't want to freak anyone out *coughs* coronavirus.

Take now, for example. Mr Hiyer did not have to make a case for us going to his colleague in Washington. He didn't have to call him and explain the backstory and implore Dr Strauss because 'I so want to help this lovely couple.' Mr Hiyer is a good guy.

So is Dr Strauss

I actually can't wait to meet him, because he and his international programme coordinator Annabel have done an amazing job of taking us under their wings already, but get this. He – and I have it on good authority – is the first person in the world to come up with a business model that, wait for it, is basically the IVF holy grail. It absolves all the emotional and financial fatigue familiar to anyone whose IVF doesn't 'work' the first time. The biggest problem – the addictive pull is all hinged on the question: when do you stop? Trying again to have your longed-for child is definitely worth another £7,000, right? Particularly if stopping means you have wasted the previous £7,000. You will have spent double, but you won't care because you'll have your baby and how do you comfortably put a finite figure on that? But then – as we've already proven – that escalates and escalates, especially if you decide to turn to surrogacy to try and win the last hand. How can you justify spending your child's inheritance on trying to create its existence, and then allow it to have all been for nothing. Wasted. The farther you go, the worse it gets, until, like us, you get, well, here.

Then there is the private medicine doubt factor, and it goes something like this: The conspiracy theorist in me reasons that of course it's in the financial interests of the private clinic to have a patient's IVF fail the first or even second time. The cruel nature of IVF lends itself to repeat custom, after all. Whereas the cash-strapped NHS would rather knock you up and ship you off as soon as medically possible. I'm not for a second suggesting private doctor sabotage is on the perfectly polished mahogany table – Mr Hiyer is based on Harley Street and I trust him implicitly – I'm just voicing my darkest suspicions, because you can't argue that where you lose, they win. And just because I'm paranoid doesn't mean they're not on their sixth yachting holiday of the summer.

Except for Dr Strauss and his shared-risk programme. It says that you can pay the 'normal' package, like we did in Miami with Dr Hernandez (although Dr Strauss' fee is around half and he has a better reputation, clinic and success rates. Argh). Or you can pay the 'more than aver-age' package, but you'd get six cycles included. Six chances to have a baby and, if it doesn't work by then, you get a 100 per cent refund. And if you're like us, you just pay it right back in and do it again. It is a simple, genius, win-win proposition. It is in his best interests to get us knocked up and shipped out the first time because he gets a bigger profit for one go. It's in our best interests because we know we can trust his advice and judgement; we know he understands how this trust issue may arise and how to get round it; and if we pay over the odds for it to work first or second time, who gives a flying fuck to be frank? We have our family; there is no losing.

OK, yes, we need to find more money, but had this been on the perfectly polished mahogany table in the beginning, we wouldn't be in these financial or emotional dire straits by now.

Where Dr Strauss is even more heroic, is that he has agreed to let us do the shared risk concept for our one and only transfer. We only have one embryo left remem-ber, so yeah, we sell our car and pay double, but it's like investing in our future. We either have a significantly (but by virtue of the outcome, insignificantly) more expensive baby, or we get our money back.

Should this last go not work over there, we have a blank slate and everything in place to bring the story home to England. When I say everything, I mean we have Rebecca. Because we don't have eggs or an egg donor in England, but to an infertile couple with no chance of personal IVF success, Rebecca is everything. Maybe we start again here and get on the UK donor waiting list. Who knows, I'm not ready to think beyond what is happening right now, and that is our third and final frozen embryo cycle with Rebecca.

Ah, Rebecca

Rebecca and Jack Randall, without whom nothing would be possible. Nothing. None of this, not this new opportunity, this way it was meant to be, this cycle that is *going* to work. It's going to, because it has to, and if (when) it does, we will owe everything to Rebecca.

Egg donor no. 234

Our anonymous donor is such an important part of this whole story – she will contribute to half of our baby's genetics after all – that I often feel quite wobbly about not knowing her. And since she signed up to forever remain anonymous, that is the way it will always stay. And then at the same time, quite secure in the knowledge that I don't know her. Because I wonder, *all the time*, about how I would cope out the other side if I did. How I would feel when I recognise her in our child's features, where I would not recognise anything of myself. It's a funny one. I try not to dwell on it too much.

Mr B, obviously

Contributor of the most absolutely important part. Ah yes, the easy part, as far as IVF medical procedures go. Don't worry, he more than makes up for it with a somewhat unrecognised supporting role: extreme project management duties and four years of emotional terror. This man is tough. I am thrilled that our child gets to inherit half of him.

But oh, it doesn't stop there. We have our exceptional lawyers, who are a literal necessity but who have gone out of their way to hold our hands throughout this incredible experience. Now we're facing a total about-turn where we won't need to enlist them in quite the same capacity, but they're still checking in all the time. Still willing us on and explaining how much easier it will be to obtain a parental order in the UK without the constraints of having to repatriate an American-born baby.

We have Emma, my gorgeous friend and incredible fertility acupuncturist, who has offered to treat Rebecca and optimise our chance of success, as enthused by Mr Hiyer, who maintains everything is better with Emma.

And then we have our obligatory counsellor, Mick, who we're sat with right now – Rebecca, Jack, Mr B and I – making sure our emotional logistics are exactly where they need to be.

There is a whole psychological element that goes hand in hand with making a baby this way. The laws around compulsory counselling are different in the UK and the USA, so even though we've already been psychologically evaluated via Skype, now we're doing it back home. We need to sit down, all together this time, and ensure we're all on the same moral page, subjectively speaking. Possible? Mick can tell us, he has a checklist on a clipboard in front of him.

It's not supremely interesting, but it's fun being in the room for the first time, all four of us, officially making this thing happen. We go over the usual stuff, you know, what happens during the birth and immediately afterwards (we'll make a proper plan when the time comes). Agreeing the 'terms' of our relationship (we look at each other and giggle at the preposterous formality of that; we're natural friends already – we're going for a drink after this), what level of contact will we maintain after the birth? Mick recommends zero contact for two weeks immediately afterwards, which I understand completely, to give us room to breathe, recover, establish boundaries after an emotionally complex scenario that will hopefully bring us to that point. I look at Rebecca and she's frowning and smirking at the same time, which I also understand completely. She's so sure she won't need space to set boundaries because as far as she's concerned, they're already set. She wants this for us, she wants the experience for herself, she doesn't want another baby and she'll feel zero ownership at any point. But I guess that's how all relationships are in the early days, full of ideals and promise and sureties. I guess Mick and his sage surrogacy advice is the equivalent of a prenuptial agreement. A gentle 'just in case, OK'? Because there is still that UK law sticking point – the one stuck firmly in my throat. Legally she has a six-week grace period after the birth to change her mind and keep the baby. Rebecca will be as prone to pregnancy hormones as the next person, right? How do we know she won't need to take some time to recover emotionally, to recalibrate back to her old pragmatic self? Of course this is something we will never say out loud to her. At this point it feels ridiculously offensive to voice our anxieties – even if some of them might seem insignificant to the common observer. Or stipulate that, yeah, even though it feels weird we probably should heed the advice and stay away just till the dust settles. That's where Mick comes in. To save us from the, 'This prenup doesn't mean I think we won't last, darling' conversation. You see? Even when you find 'the one', surrogacy can still be a bit, well, sticky.

We know with our whole hearts that Rebecca and Jack are our ones, though. We go for a drink straight after the session and it has all the potential to be somewhat uncomfortable. We just had group therapy with two people we basically just met, and I guess I feel a bit like we're all naked now, sitting here in this pub. Awkward! Rebecca is the first to break the ice, of course, by telling me exactly what I'm thinking. 'We can work out how we feel about keeping contact in those two weeks later down the line. I'm not worried about me for a second, but I get that you might want some time on your own to bond.' She's so right. And I have no idea how I'll feel in nine months. She finishes her pineapple juice while the rest of us sip our stronger alternatives and ends by saying, 'But first, let's get pregnant!'

And so, we shall. Or at least, we shall try. Again.

Because it's time to get started. This is our mission entirely possible, and the plan goes like this: Mr B and I have almost finished badgering all the lackadaisical relevant parties into coordinating our old paperwork so we can get our embryo released from Miami to Dr Strauss' Washington lab. All being well it will begin its merry journey next week. Good luck little one, *bonnes vacances*, have a safe flight for the love of all that is holy.

Rebecca will start her IVF preparatory cycle tomorrow – hence the pineapple juice – and if she responds in the way the planets aligned for us, she and I will fly to Washington in three short weeks to give our last-chance embryo it's very best chance.

This has been a meeting of medical minds, a logistical nightmare that turned into a dream come true, and because everything feels so perfectly, wonderfully right, I can feel my hopes getting so dangerously high they have altitude sickness. But I'm not going to pay that any mind right now; it is what it is, I can't muster enough energy to even try and control my emotions. So, OK swan song, let's do this.

16.

How do you stay positive?

Back when I had cancer and I'd travel to the hospital every three weeks for my chemotherapy, I got to know the nurses who administered my medication quite well. They were kind and funny and helped me while away the hours in that one place I would least like to be in the world at that time. Except for one day, when a new nurse came in to cover a shift and basically destroyed my sanity with one deft conversation. I was feeling blue, quite ill and I'd had some scary test results swiftly followed by the devastating news I'd need a mastectomy. She told me it was really important to stay positive. I needed to hear some solid, life-affirming advice, so I clung onto every morsel she offered me. 'Because there are two types of people who go through cancer; I've seen it so many times. Type A, who stay really positive and believe they can beat it and never wallow in doubt or fear. Or type B, who are pessimistic, who resign themselves to this terrible thing happening to them and aren't strong enough not to be negative.' OK, I'm trying! I thought. She continued, 'And no one who is a type B survives.'

Holy fuck lady. You try remaining positive at all times when you're about to lose a boob to save your life at age thirty. And then try to maintain it when you've just been told that if you slip into negative thoughts you will die anyway. I mean, come on. I was terrified for the next four months of treatment. Too afraid of my thoughts to risk going to sleep in case negativity crept into my subconscious. It was already there, of course, this self-perpetuating lunacy that a nurse had just lumbered me with – an impossible catch-22. It was also nonsense because here I am, ten years later, trying to have a baby, and I definitely didn't manage positivity the whole time.

It is useful though, that way of thinking. It does help pep your mood somewhat. And now that my scenario isn't literally life or death, I feel a bit more positive about trying to stay positive. Except that our odds aren't so great, though. Fifty-fifty in fact, according to Dr Strauss, who is refreshingly no-nonsense, but still. I was hoping for more. Mostly because with donor eggs and surrogacy, it's *usually* more. Especially given how we're doing it – controlling the variables in such an optimum way – meaning you're usually looking at around a seventy per cent success rate. And then, on top of that, we added in pre-genetic diagnosis (where we biopsied the embryos to make sure they were chromosomally perfect), and this last time, on the advice of Dr Strauss and Mr Hiyer, an ERA (another biopsy, this time of Rebecca's uterus to work out the exact right time to do the transfer). Oh, and we have Emma's magical acupuncture and Rebecca's commitment to eating healthily and exercising as advised. *Surely* we're looking at around the high nineties by then. Nope. Just your plain old average 50:50.

The hypothetical problem is that we are bashing the same drum as it were. Sure, in Rebecca we have a new person wielding the drumstick, but we have a glaring UNKNOWN REASON FOR PAST FAILURES warning flashing above our heads. Our past failures have been statistical oddities, dammit, so the likelihood is there's something wrong somewhere. And the most likely place is a 'bad egg'. My dad, who has been obsessing about all this accumulative bad news just as much as I have, took an opportunity to bypass all the medical information we've collated and ask my husband directly what his theory on it always going wrong was. He didn't wait for an answer before he offered his, 'I'm worried about your sperm.'

But no, Dad. His sperm is better than fine, but I'm sure he really relished having that conversation with his father-in-law over a cup of tea in the kitchen. No, this is basically another US agency transgression, I'm afraid. Back when we were enlisting them for our surrogacy journey, and we were green and eager and had nothing but trust in the system, we excitedly signed up for their in-house donor egg programme. Now, as we languish in all this hindsight, we have some serious worries about their protocol. All of us do. Dr Strauss in particular is disappointed that our chosen donor has never had her own pregnancy, but also none of her donated eggs have ever resulted in a pregnancy, meaning she isn't a proven successful egg donor. It sounds mercenary, when you put it like that, but it would have been great to have known this was even a thing back when we were starting out. We had no idea it was something to ask about, let alone avoid, but, you live and learn, eh? We've certainly done a lot of both of those things by now. So yes, after all of this, we're left with the possibility that our donor eggs are just not great, and this last embryo, that is winging its way to Washington as we speak, has a bad reputation because of its poor defeated siblings. And oh, the paranoia that creeps in too. Mr B and I have had enough sleepless nights worrying about the care taken over the transport of that embryo. Granted the lack of sleep might have contributed to the worry, until we were in the midst of a vicious cycle of stress, but since we obviously pissed off Dr Hernandez, what if he 'forgot' to turn the freezer on properly? What if he contaminated the test tube? What if he sent someone else's embryo? What if we get some rational thought back on the table and concentrate on worrying about the things we *do* know, instead of where our wild imagination takes us?

Whilst I struggle to remain positive, I am inordinately lucky that I have a whole other partner now who is unwaveringly so. Rebecca's attitude to this means I'm not too worried about disrupting the universe's plans for me with my negative thoughts, but still, I try to keep up with her. I pretend. I keep going. I work hard and I distract myself. But I'm pretending, nonetheless. Especially at work, where I feel I can't let anyone in on the trauma playing out in my personal background. Oh no. That would be wholly unprofessional, right? I am not someone who cries in the boardroom, as it were. Except that time right after my infertility diagnosis where I actually did, literally, cry in the boardroom. When I shut myself in so no one else would see me till I calmed down, only it was entirely made of glass, and the rest of my *ELLE* magazine team were just outside, totally seeing me. So yes, now I hold it down till I get home. I don't recommend this as a viable coping strategy, but it's mine and I guess it works for me. I'm lucky that I have a job that I adore, and distracting myself with my work is enough to remind me that there is life outside baby making. And it's quite nice in itself actually – look how fulfilled I am right now, that I just pulled off a presentation that made the room actually clap at my ideas. Maybe I don't need a baby after all, you know, if this were all to go fundamentally wrong in the end. Maybe I just work so hard that I don't notice I have a gaping space in my heart. That is how I stay positive at work.

At home, however, it's a different matter, because my husband is as deep into our backstory as I am, because obviously it's his burden too. At home, there is no pretending, so we have a different kind of task at hand, and that is to keep each other positive instead. How do you do that when you're feeling absolutely heartbroken, and looking at the other person makes you feel worse because you can see it reflected back at you? Plus you feel guilty because you can't fulfil the one thing that would make this person you love feel better? Fucked if I know, to be perfectly honest. This is the hard part, and we haven't worked it out, but we haven't tried to either. It just happens, because no one within our four walls needs another emotional project to master. It seems we both break down quite hard and quite frequently, but somehow, never at the same time. This is the key to keeping going, because it means we are very good at propping each other up. Like last week, for instance, when Mr B was feeling despondent, blue, pessimistic, all of the things that frequent our mind space on a daily basis. He told me on this occasion, so I spent a couple of hours reinforcing how brilliant the possibility of this last chance working with Rebecca is, actually. How fifty-fifty is fantastic odds because we're due some winning luck by now. How we have the same chance of it working as not working, and there is absolutely no reason whatsoever to believe it won't work. There just isn't! So it *could* work, couldn't it? By the end of the conversation we were both recalibrated. We were buzzing on the possibility of success, and what our future, or even just what our living room, would look like with a little person in it. It was thrilling and lovely. And then the next day it wasn't. I faltered. Stopped believing my own hype, had the sickening fear of the other side of the coin that meant all of the things we'd fantasised about the night before were completely out of reach, and so I just crumpled and cried quietly until Mr B came to find me. Then it was his turn, and he

252

turned it around by presenting a different perspective and this, dear friends, is how a perpetually unlucky couple keep on trucking in the face of constant failure. It is all about the reinforcements, and I'm lucky that I have my own personal army. I know not everyone is so heavily supported. Knowing Mr B has taught me that.

My dad is called Jos and he is … Well, he's … Um, it's quite hard to articulate a feeling of unconditional love, isn't it? He's a nightmare, a lot of the time, in a way that dads tend to be. Often embarrassing, wildly inappropriate, stubborn in a head-of-the-family way, and voraciously, indignantly right *all the time*. But the thing is he *is* right a lot of the time, and he's taken such good care of me that I feel secure just thinking about him. Basically, to me he is perfection in father form. And he has suffered through this whole experience with me, like it has been happening to him – because in a way I suppose it has. He and my mum are the people I call when I'm having a panic attack, even if Mr B is in the next room, so needless to say they've had a lot of involvement in this particular Mother Project.

My mum Jane is the perfect counter to my dad, which is probably why their marriage has lasted for just shy of fifty years. She is my rock and my role model and she would totally cringe at such a platitude, but it's true even without either of us acknowledging it till I just wrote it down. My mum and I are so similar in our values, our looks, even our fingernails, which I love because I will always be able to think of her when I simply glance at my own hands. She is exactly the mother I aspire to be: supremely nurturing but pragmatic, realistic. She's the most comforting person I can think of, but she'd bolster me to get through things my own way, too. I suspect it's why I'm able to deal with this hand I'm dealt right now. We're dealt, I should say.

I can't think about how it must have hurt my parents to receive the call from Mr B that their youngest daughter had breast cancer. It's the darkest part of my remembering of that whole experience, and something I have struggled to address even in therapy, so I am unequipped to address it here. I can only hope that one day I do understand that kind of love and attachment from their perspective, because I will be bringing up their grandchild. But without the cancer part, OK universe? We've all been through quite enough, thank you.

My big sister Amy represents what I want from my life, but she would be flabbergasted to know that. We've often been diametrically opposed growing up, because isn't that an affliction of so many siblings? We have different ambitions and relationships and attitudes. She has pink hair and multiple tattoos that she half-heartedly fails to hide from our parents. And she hates wine for goodness' sake! But she has these two beautiful, hilarious daughters and she is a downright fantastic mother to them – so much so that I sort of forget she was just my sister before she was their mum. I think I am so obsessed with Christmas because it's when we're all together. And the excessive consumption of Quality Street, of course.

But like I said, some, like my husband, are not quite so lucky.

One great quality about Mr B is that he has always made time to listen to people when he knows they need him to, and he has a good sense for that. He also has a lot of difficult and fantastically interesting worldly experience under his belt, so he's good for imparting wisdom when he sees fit, especially to those he cares about. The sad part as I see it is that it often doesn't go both ways. Mr B's extended family – once very close – is now fractured for various reasons, including divorce, parental absence, tangled politics and the sad et cetera that means he's had to get by with a reduced service since he was young.

It's when we go through the tough times together – like now – that I see how much he doesn't have that something that I'm so sure of I almost take it for granted. Where I readily call on my troops when I need them, Mr B has done most of his combat alone.

This might be helpful when it comes to wondering how to support someone on a similar track of grief, disappointment, grief, repeat, but here's what I think. Support is picking up the phone when the text goes unanswered. Support is checking in every other day to see how they're feeling, because if they seem fine today, they might not be fine tomorrow. It's trying and keeping trying, basically, because sometimes people who need your help the most might be resistant as first defence.

I wish Mr B still had his mum. She was resolutely stubborn when it came to her son. She would call and not stop calling from her home in Ireland, even when their relationship went through some very turbulent times. She sadly died before she knew we were trying for a family. She isn't here to offer him the comfort that he needs right now. As such he's pretty much made his own way through life, and I know our child will be better off because of what he's taught himself. But my advice for anyone who might come up against a seemingly strong person you love who you think is doing fine without you is this: it is within your power to keep chipping away at the wall, because there's someone on the other side who has built it precisely because they need you.

And then, of course, there's that other thing about surrogacy that means we have a whole gang where most people just have each other. Collectively we are the Take That to your Robbie Williams. No one can really say who was more successful, but there are definite bonuses to going out on stage with a band to back you up.

Ours is a curious four-way symbiotic relationship. And it is particularly important and complicated right now, because Rebecca has started treatment and we have a date set for the transfer. So far so relatively simple, right? So come on then, what gives? Oh, OK, so probably her medication protocol isn't going to be particularly effective first time, so it's alright, just means we need to give it a little more time and— hang on, news just in, Rebecca is on the WhatsApp:

> Mr Hiyer said everything looked exactly as he wanted it to be.

> Wait, what?

> Lining is 10–12 mm.

Oh! My goodness! Well we weren't expecting that, just because we've learnt not to. Next up is the start of the progesterone injections, the necessary and crucial part of this cycle that helps maintain the thickness of the lining. And they're probably going to— oh wait, it's Rebecca again.

> Injections are totally fine! You're going to have to do the ones in Washington though Sophie because I can't reach where I need to inject them on my own.

GULP. But OK!

'Oh easy,' I lie, so she doesn't worry, but I'm actually quite worried.

Rebecca is easily clearing every hurdle we've previously fallen at, and I'm not quite sure I comprehend. This is going *right* so far. Zero complications! Except we have to book flights now, only after we knew the transfer was definitely OK to go ahead based on the scan results, and they're probably going to be extortionate. Well, now I'm just looking for hurdles where they don't exist. The plane tickets are fine, and who cares anyway? They're taking us straight to our potential future baby and everything is just clicking neatly into place like it – dare I say it – like it was meant to be. I actually daren't, because the bigger part of me is holding back on the optimism here. Since Rebecca and I have become closer, simply by virtue of being two empathetic women collaborating on one womb (it makes for quite a special bonding experience), I message her on our own chat outside of the group WhatsApp.

I'm so scared of hoping it'll work.

She pings me back within seconds.

Don't worry, I'll do it for you.

Does she mean she'll do the hoping or she'll do the 'it'. The whole thing? She'll bring it home?

It doesn't matter in the end, it's just a lovely thing to say, and so you see? I wonder if she thinks it will definitely work, or if she's trying to keep us positive, or both, but whatever, she's manifesting unwavering positivity that means whatever happens, we're going to survive. We're type A.

17.
What is the transfer like?

Well this transfer is both unlike any other transfer there ever was, but also exactly the damn same. It's different because, including my own five attempts at getting pregnant, it's our eighth. Our eighth! We are those people. That couple who mindlessly kept going and kept going, acquiring an ever more depressing conglomeration of catastrophes so that we arrived here, weary and very heavily laden with excess baggage. It's different because it's our last chance. I wish I could change the record, but it's true. And it's mega, so I can't, I'm afraid. 'Tis what it is. And 'tis the end of the embryo-road. And it's different because a) we have Rebecca, so even though we're doing the transfer in America, we're doing the pregnancy (come on pregnancy!) in England, and b) so far, so good.

It's the same because technically these things follow a medical protocol and it's largely the same whether you do it with a cancer-incapacitated patient in Russia, a paid American surrogate in Miami, or an angel altruistic Brit in Washington, and first things first, no, it doesn't hurt. In fact, it's really quite wonderful, whatever brings you to the room. Even if it's your eighth time.

An embryo transfer takes about five minutes all in, but it's five minutes of pure abundant hope that is scary, yes – there's no getting around it – but also thrilling. This one is going to feel more like seventy-two hours because I'm on my way to meet Rebecca at the airport, and it's just the two of us, flying to the Washington clinic to please, please bring our baby home. For me, it starts now.

Except I'm so sure I've jinxed it already and we're only fifteen minutes into the car journey. A couple of days ago I was with my parents at home, and Dad snuck off upstairs to get me something. 'I have this gold mezuzah that I was given by my father when I was thirteen,' he says. Oh yes! I suddenly have a rush of memories of him wearing it throughout my childhood – this smart little cylinder on a short gold chain that I had no idea had any significance until now. He holds out his hand and there it is, exactly how I remembered. It's a hollow chamber, meant to hold a tiny rolled-up parchment containing specific verses from the Torah. Traditionally they're placed on the doorframe outside a house, but this one he's always worn around his neck, and now he's written 'Mazel Tov' and a smiley face on a tiny piece of paper, rolled it up and placed it carefully inside. 'I want you to have a piece of me there with you, for good luck. You've never had that before, so this time it's going to be different.' Well, if that's not enough to tear through a fragile, hopeful heart, I don't know what is. I put it on immediately and I vow not to take it off, maybe ever again. I'm wearing it now in fact, rolling it between my finger and thumb to comfort me while my heart races with the enormity of what this trip represents. There's a tiny hole carved out near the top, a little like a whistle, and when I glance down I realise there's no flash of white showing through. Sure enough, it's empty. My dad's handwritten note isn't nestled in the tube where he placed it, it must have fallen out somewhere, and I'm devastated. I'm so sure that this is a bad omen, that I've ruined my chance because he said I was taking a part of him with me for good luck, and now I've carelessly lost it. I call him in floods of tears at not even six in the morning and try to explain my superstitious certainty to him.

'Oh for goodness' sake Sophiepops,' he says. 'It's just a silly piece of paper! You have the necklace, you know I'll be there with you in spirit.'

I'm hooking the likelihood of this embryo transfer being successful on a tiny scrap of sentimental handwriting. This is where years of infertility struggling gets you. So come on Sophiepops, it's only a silly piece of paper.

To be honest, I've been nervous about this trip, for reasons outside of the obvious, for a while, so I spend the rest of the car journey focusing on those instead. Even though the circumstances of mine and Rebecca's relationship mean that I basically love her already, we still don't know each other very well if you really break it down. Certainly not 'girls' holiday' well, anyway. Trips away are always supposed to be a test, aren't they? They tend to induce some kind of make-or-break conclusion, and this thing we all have is way too delicate and important to undergo that kind of pressure. Granted it's only three days, and one of them will be spent in a fertility clinic, so it's not your run-of-the-mill jaunt, but I'm still way too preoccupied with my nerves. What will we even talk about on a nine-hour flight? Will it be awkward, or stilted, the first time we're on our own and in such close proximity for such a length of time? How will we fill all the time in between movies – crosswording? Also, I'm a really bad flyer. The first thing I do when we sit down in our seats is warn Rebecca that she might have to hold my hand, and that I might have a panic attack. And that I've downloaded an itinerary of funny movies for the flight and the hotel stay, in case there aren't any good ones, because laughing apparently might help the embryo implant. That's it. I've totally lost the plot. But the way I see it, we've tried everything – the Western medicine way, the Eastern, the alternative, the text book and forum-following. Why not rely on a bit of laughter to bring it home this time?

Rebecca is the absolute sweetest. She produces a pair of matching slippers that she's bought for the flight and that I will now treasure forever. They're fluffy, sequin animal print and are so perfectly mood-boosting in that moment that I want to cry. Which could also be the fear settling in.

This apparently non-emotional pragmatist sitting next to me is going a long way to undoing her steely reputation, because now she's proffering me a sealed letter, written by her Aunt Sallie, one for her, one for me, that we've been instructed not to read till we're on the plane. Rebecca can't wait till we take off, she's impatient like that – so we open them both and try not to cry. There are two red string bracelets inside with magic eyes for good luck, and the loveliest words of encouragement that make me feel like part of the family. There is so much love surrounding our little crew that I can almost feel it seeping into my luggage, ready to come with us to Washington.

And the flight is – I can't believe I'm saying this about a plane journey, but – it's *fun*! Having nine straight hours just us is the best thing, actually. We just solidify our solidarity, in between movies. No crosswording necessary! We sync our films so we know what the other is laughing at at the same time. We eat the disgusting food and chat as easily as I would with any of my close friends, and we watch Jack's instructional video on how to correctly inject his wife in her 'flank', which frankly is funnier than any of the movies. But I totally get it. His wife is in my care for the next few days and he probably has a similar level of anxiety about entrusting her to me – virtual stranger, ostensibly met on the internet – as I do. Especially since I have to puncture her skin with a needle as soon as we get to the hotel room. We have a strict window for that and I'm really not looking forward to it. Oh man, I'm nervous again.

* * *

The fertility clinic and lab is situated in a kind of medical industrialised part of town. There are huge wide roads with massive square buildings at several cross junctions, and literally nothing else in between except manicured grass and sidewalks. It feels like a very serious kind of trading estate but less shops, more medical and educational facilities. Our hotel is just across the street from the clinic, and as we unload our hand luggage and prepare to check in, I have a sudden moment of overwhelming love. I can see the building that contains our embryo. The crazy part is that it's been cryogenically frozen for well over a year already, suspended in time. I know it's not a person yet, but in my head it totally is, and by all rights it should have celebrated its first birthday already, but instead there it is, just right over there, waiting for us to make it real. We take a quick picture of us with the building in the background for posterity, and send it to the WhatsApp group chat with 'There it is behind us.' It's quite amazing to be here, on the doorstep of this place that we've talked about incessantly, that we've leveraged to heroic saviour status. But when I look at the picture, I can see that my smile doesn't quite reach my eyes. Mr B must see it too because he pings me on the side and says, 'I'm so proud of you.'

'I haven't done anything,' is my common response. My surrogacy mantra, that sort of pokes the bruise in a weirdly relieving way. Like if I say it I'm addressing the elephant in the room, the fact I'm more of a third wheel in the process than a key component. Just for now. When the baby comes, I'm straight in at No. 1, but in the meantime it feels as though I'm limping into the charts at best. But I don't say it this time because, yeah, I'm quite proud of me, too. I'm struggling inside, but I don't want Rebecca to feel anything other than wonderful, so I promise myself I won't let her see. And in doing that, I won't let myself know how hard this is either. The enormity of what this last mini trip will or won't deliver. The impact it will have on our entire future and the part I can't bear to even think about on the other side of this next Two Week Wait. I'll bury it, I'll conjure the excitement and hope that is sitting just beneath my panic, and I'll focus on that instead. Deep breaths, deeeep breaths.

The hotel is perfectly perfunctory – this is Healthcare Hill after all. There is nothing fancy to be found among such a concentration of medical offices and facilities, but I booked us the nicest rooms I could find and so we settle in and then we set about clearing out the bad juju. Oh, uh huh, you heard me right – we are absolutely leaving no spiritual stone unturned. My friend Emma the acupuncturist packed us off with a gift box containing sage to burn in our hotel room, and palo santo to anoint each other with. I hear you muttering; I don't care, we're doing it. After I've done the thing I've been dreading the most in this lead-up. Injecting another person in the bottom, in case you're not a nurse or other qualified professional, is really quite terrifying. It goes against instinct, especially if you're a recovering needle-phobe, like me. I've recovered because during my chemotherapy and then my own IVF I've had to pierce myself in the thigh or stomach so many times I've lost count and, believe me, that took a lot of getting used to. But doing it to someone else entirely? Well that's a whole other ball game. I have had to pretend I'm totally cool with this whole thing this whole time, because the last thing Rebecca needs to know is that my hands are shaking as I load the syringe with the pre-measured dose of progesterone. God, why am I shaking? This is ridiculous. I also cannot afford to get it wrong, because our future baby's life depends on it, literally. This is the last dose before the transfer and it is necessary for it to all go ahead. Woah, this needle is bigger than I remember when I did it. No, it's definitely bigger. I'm going to cause this person some pain now, but it's for the greater good, so I shut my eyes – kidding, of course I don't do that, I need to see where I'm putting this thing – and I talk through what I'm doing as if I were in fact trained in this fine art. Those famous four words they surely teach at nursing school: 'OK, ready? Sharp scratch!' And then it's done. We're both totally relieved. We light our sage, clear any lingering negative energy, and go to bed. Tomorrow is a big day. The biggest so far, in fact.

It's the next day and Rebecca is having a final scan before the transfer to make sure that everything is at its absolute optimum. Only Dr Strauss is frowning. Yes, that's definitely a frown. I feel cold dread drip slowly through my ribcage and settle somewhere near my stomach. There's a terribly long pause, then he looks at Rebecca and shakes his head while he explains that her womb lining has inexplicably disappeared to nothing, seemingly overnight, and so the transfer can't go ahead.

I open my eyes and realise that, THANK GOD, I'm still in my hotel bed and, of course, I was having the world's most realistic and relevant nightmare just before I roused myself from REM sleep. For Christ's sake, this is ridiculous. I am ridiculously anxious, even when I'm unconscious.

Phew! OK, so I'm still here. It's still the morning of final embryo transfer day, and Rebecca is also still in her room. We've made a plan to meet for breakfast so we can take the edge off any Big Day nerves and experience every part of it together. As I lie in bed and wait for my alarm to go off, I do a comparison scan against the five times I woke up on my own embryo transfer days in Russia. That was a much nicer hotel room, but the big bonus here is that I'm allowed to drink coffee this time. Also, I don't have that familiar anxiety about my body letting us all down. I realise that poor Rebecca would probably be feeling that instead. There's a huge weight of responsibility that comes with surrogacy, but we have always done everything to try to relieve her of as much of it as we can.

When I knock on Rebecca's door, she opens it beaming. She's totally fine, flushed cheeks – most likely exhilarated – and she's clutching all of her transfer notes in her hands, telling me she's been up for ages, double checking the paperwork to make sure she's doing everything right. God I love her.

Our transfer appointment is only half an hour away and so Rebecca downs the last of her litre bottle of water and we make our way out of the hotel, across the road to the clinic to finally meet Dr Strauss.

As we walk into the medical centre, I find myself thinking of our last surrogate, Lydia, imagining her doing this all by herself, for me, while Mr B and I agonised at home waiting for every update. It's amazing to actually be here this time; it's like we're totally in it together. I wonder if things would have been different had I known Lydia in person, in proximity. And it makes my heart pang with retrospective gratitude, even though it didn't end quite as nicely as it started. She still tried to carry a baby for me, that part is irrefutable. I haven't even stepped over the threshold and I'm already welling up at the thought of everything that has brought us to this point. Oh my goodness, it's going to be a long day.

The clinic is, of course, immaculate and impressive in that American-hospital way that British people slather over. I am indeed slathering. Why can't our hospital walls be painted this colour? Why can't we have tasteful carpet and a voluminous floral display in our reception halls? It's like gynaecology Disneyland and Rebecca and I are open-mouthed as we're ushered into Annabel's office to do some admin before we meet Dr Strauss. God, she's lovely. Annabel has helped facilitate every part of this hostage-rescue operation with such elegant precision that we've felt cared for and safe from the moment she picked up the phone. She's warm and welcoming and so, so thrilled to be able to help that her smile is practically cracking her face in two. Although surrogacy is substantially more common in America than it is in England, I guess we're still somewhat exotic. For one, I've been writing about our efforts in a national newspaper, and for another, our surrogate is altruistic, which is obviously a real rarity in the States. It instantly makes her more appealing, doesn't it? She's so easy to like anyway, but take the customary commercial fee requirement out of the running, and she is positively angelic. Dr Strauss comes to pick us up from Annabel's office himself, and greets us like we're golfing buddies. He has a charming smile and is so affable it throws me off guard. He's a renowned physician, his job is miraculous, but he's jovial and relaxed as if we're meeting for a quick coffee, rather than to create new life.

First things first, he told us the embryo had thawed *perfectly*. Perfectly! 'We like to see around 80 per cent cells and yours saw 95–100 per cent.' I still don't really know what that means, but I feel what I can only describe as pre-parental pride. I can feel myself going again. 'But, [No! Not a "but"!] I want to manage your expectations.' He doesn't need to worry about managing my expectations. They are micromanaged to the point they want to hand in their resignation, but I'm still a little sad to have to focus on the doubt right now. He reminds us that the last two unexplained failures mean he has no idea which way this one is going to go. Rebecca, unjaded by a tumultuous series of failures thus far, tells us both, 'Well, every time an embryo has been in there before, it's stuck first time.' She means both times she and Jack tried for a baby they fell pregnant straight away, so she is of the firm assumption this will be no different. It's enough to make me hope so too, and that is about the best I can muster right now. I'm supremely grateful to her for that.

And then it's time. We're both led down a corridor to a little set of lockers where we find our hospital scrubs and plastic hygiene booties. I travelled all the way to Washington to give Rebecca all the support she needed, to look after her for Jack, and to be right next to the action as it were, but I hadn't actually thought about being in the room for the transfer until she told me to come in. The clinic has two hospital bracelets ready, one for each of us, which is a seemingly tiny detail, but does *everything* to make me feel significant in this moment. The whiteboard on the wall has both of our names and dates of birth, as if we're two people, one patient. Which I guess we are! The two women collectively comprising the 'mother' part of this particular Mother Project: Rebecca in the societally accepted semantic sense, and me in the hopefully-soon-to-be one.

The nurse who affixed our bracelets leaves the room and we both do a little polite dance as it becomes clear Rebecca now needs to assume the position, as it were. Oh um, well. Obviously, I am far too British to say what we're both thinking, that it's quite an, ahem, intimate procedure, isn't it? Not one you'd usually do with a new friend in the room. During the course of our relationship we haven't even hugged for longer than is strictly necessary, and now here I am assuring her I'll obviously be staying at the head end. Rebecca seems totally unfazed, and I have to remind myself that she's had two babies already. I understand your modesty concerns change somewhat once you've been through childbirth.

I smuggled my phone in – oops, sorry Doc, but there are four of us in this alliance, and one in particular is on absolute tenterhooks back home. As such, my phone keeps pinging. It's Mr B of course, but he keeps texting to ask if *I'm* OK. And he's right on the money, because I haven't really asked myself that question yet. I appreciate that he sees that this might be strange for me; to actually watch this lovely woman try to do what I couldn't manage to do myself, for us. I tell him I am completely great and I really mean it. Bone-achingly nervous and still slightly panicky, yes. Never for a moment allowing myself to believe this one is going to stick, because if I do that and it doesn't, I think I might actually shatter. But right now, here with Rebecca, and feeling the quite percipient support from him back home, totally great.

Argh, Dr Strauss just walked in, this time in full-on scrubs and surgical gloves, hands held aloft as if he's about to perform a TV operation, but he sets the tone like this is completely normal and easy, an absolutely everyday occurrence. Which, of course, to him it is. He smiles at us both, tells me to watch the screen behind Rebecca's head, and then explains that what we're looking at is an ultrasonic image of Rebecca's womb and, look, now he is gently feeding the catheter into the uterine cavity. See? There it goes!

There's a guy standing just to his left, holding a plastic syringe with a thin long tube attached. Inside there, according to my previous experience, is our defrosted embryo. It's so mad to me that my future baby – toddler, teenager – fits in that tiny tube, and I can't stop looking at the guy just standing there holding it like it's just his job, just another embryo. Doesn't he know how important this one is? He passes the whole thing to Dr Strauss who then feeds the tube into the catheter, and then points back at the screen, and – whoosh! A tiny light is sort of flushed into view, as he discharges it out to where it hopefully needs to be. I'm awestruck as ever during these moments. Everything in this room just changed. Everything! In the space of that one very short appointment, there might be a whole new life trying to happen, right now, as we stare at the screen. As I stare at the screen and Rebecca beams at me and Dr Strauss stands up with a, 'Well, that was a very easy transfer, exactly what we want.' And then he is gone.

I really, *really* want to cry and damn it, my eyes are dry. Mostly because I've been on the verge of tears all day and I feel like I need the release. Also, because that's what would be expected of me I think, it's what I expected of myself anyway because it's what you do at times like these, isn't it? Sob and clutch each other and take shuddering breaths, etc. So what's wrong with me? Am I so jaded that I don't feel anymore? Or – and I suspect this is more likely – is it way too surreal to properly process right now and it'll hit me later, when I'm back at home and doing the laundry probably, or in a work meeting, which would be suitably mortifying. What I can feel right now is a confusing jumble of extreme pride, love, sadness, hope, wonder and panic. I want to kiss Rebecca, but she hasn't got any knickers on, so that would be entirely inappropriate. Instead I squeeze her shoulder and say, 'Well done!' when what I mean is, 'I CAN'T BELIEVE YOU JUST DID ALL THAT, FOR ME! (in my head I'm shouting). And I LOVE YOU.'

What she says is, 'Oh my God, can I go to the toilet yet?', because her bladder is full to bursting from all the water she was instructed to drink before the transfer. It makes for a clearer ultrasound, but it also makes for a horrendously uncomfortable five-minute wait before she can get up and go. I help her up, turn to face the wall while she gets dressed again and then we walk out of the room, the three of us this time.

'It's weird to say, but hoping this will work honestly feels the same as hoping I'll win the lottery. That's how unlikely it feels.' We're strolling to a celebratory dinner a little way out of town that Rebecca's lovely parents are treating us too. It's wonderfully warming how her whole family has embraced this experience. It's making me a little homesick, in fact.

Rebecca doesn't miss a beat, and says, 'Well I think it's worked already, so there.'

I think she's being kind, but a little spark ignites in me. What if? What if she knows and can feel it already? Science tells me it takes about 48 to 72 hours for an embryo to implant, and so far it's been five, but you never know, eh? Well yes, yes you do know, that's what science is there for, but I shake my head and appreciate her type-A positive stance. It's so lovely and so encouraging.

We spent the afternoon adhering to a carefully planned itinerary of maximum implantation optimisation. First we ordered Philly cheesesteak sandwiches and ate them on Rebecca's hotel bed. Options are quite limited out here, so we went for the 'comfort food is good for the soul' philosophy. One point to us. Then we sat and watched a funny film because, remember, laughing might help up the chance of implantation. According to, um, OK I can't remember, but laughing is as good for the soul as the Philly cheesesteak, so maybe it's all good for the uterus too. The film actually wasn't funny – it's difficult to find anything amusing under these highly charged circumstances – but Rebecca, bless her, laughed heartily at even the most unfunny parts, so then I did too. Ah, the sweet chorus of two desperate women forcing the fun out of quite a tense situation. Then, and this is where we are surely winning this thing, we made dream catchers, to catch our dream, duh. Rebecca had schlepped her glue

gun 3,700 miles so that we could craft for calmness. I'm
so glad she did, because it is genuinely the most soothing
way to pass the time. Mr B FaceTimed at the beginning
to check up on us, and then spent an hour just sat watching from London. We forgot he was there, that's how
intensely we crafted this afternoon. And now it's dinner
time, only we're too full of hope and love and Philly
cheesesteaks to make the most of the menu.

When we get back to the hotel and go our separate
ways to bed, I don't know what to do with myself. We're
just on opposite sides of the corridor but this feels sort of
like we've been cleaved apart. I didn't particularly want
to say goodnight, but I think it's because I'm suddenly
acutely aware that she might have my baby in her belly.
I've totally come to terms with that being the case – of
course I have or we wouldn't be able to even be here.
This isn't a feeling of jealousy, more separation anxiety,
or something similar. It's just that I'm already quite
attached to that embryo and, well, I left it. In someone
else's possession across the corridor. I said something
bumbling like 'Take good care of our baby!' and then I
got in my room and kicked myself. Like I was suggesting
she wouldn't? There are so many levels of mutual sensi-
tivity to trip up on. Was she lying awake worrying about
me worrying? Argh, we should've just bunked together
and be done with it.

Apparently I wasn't too wound up because I was
asleep within about three seconds – a soporific combination of jetlag, emotional tidal waves and comfort-eating

– and then BZZZZZZZ BZZZZZZZZZ, my alarm is going off, alerting me to the fact it is time to get up and go home.

It feels like a poignant moment, stood outside the hotel, waving goodbye to the clinic that just changed our lives for better or for worse. We've only been here for forty-eight hours but that's like two weeks in IVF world, so it's a kind of sweet sorrow to see the back of it already. All that planning and engineering and negotiating and now it's just us – Rebecca and me – on our way our second long-haul plane journey in as many days.

We flew out as a two and are coming back a three. I spend most of the flight reasoning with myself that the air pressure has no effect on my embryo in there. Not my body, not biologically possible either. It's just not how the uterus works, but still, if there is something to worry about in this scenario, I will find it. It's Rebecca's birthday mid-flight, so I give her the present I've been agonising over for weeks. What the hell do you gift the woman who is trying to give you the world? A personalised bracelet? With a meaningful message and carefully considered colourway that talks to the superstitious spiritualist side of both of us? I hope she loves it, because I can't explain how wonderful I think she is so I want her to know it. Rebecca is not one for schmultzy shows of affection. It's what she believes makes her the perfect candidate for surrogacy. But still, I'm determined to show it. Hah!

I'm doing really well until we get about two hours from Heathrow and I suddenly feel so grateful for all the people who hold me up that I badly want to be at home with them, and I feel overwhelmingly homesick. I know I'm almost there, that home is so near now, but I think I kind of let go of all this build-up and tension. It's been such a mission and I realise that once we get off this plane, that's it. There's nothing more I can do. But then, ha HA! There was *never* anything I could do. It's just down to luck at this point, isn't it? Only we haven't had so much of that in the past, so I guess the question is will our trend continue, or is this where the tables turn and everything changes. I'm not sure I'm ready to find out. I'm not sure. But we're here. We are home.

18.
How do you know when to stop?

Well, we are PUPO as the forums say, Pregnant Until Proven Otherwise, and we'll remain calm over this next Two Week Wait, OK? Cool as a cucumber, wallowing in serenity and meditative thoughts. Ahaa. Ha ha.

We are absolutely 100 per cent kidding ourselves that we will have a back-up plan should this very last chance fail, but the truth of the matter is that neither Mr B nor I feel we can keep doing this to ourselves. It's not just the money, and believe me when I say that ran out a while ago, it's the turmoil. Anyone who has been or is going through IVF will attest to the fact that it is bone-jan-glingly stressful, even if it goes right the first time. It's also fantastic and progressive and wildly exciting, don't get me wrong, but my goodness the accumulative anxiety is hard to cope with. I have a friend who took one roll of the dice a few years ago. She had a great result, six healthy embryos, and just like that fell pregnant on her first go. Sadly though, her positive result didn't last past four weeks, and she found the whole experience so trau-matising that she immediately knew she couldn't do it again. She donated her remaining embryos and she and her husband now live a totally different life to the one they imagined for themselves, but they bloody love it. There's something to be said for being unencumbered by years of sadness, ripping off the plaster and letting the air get to the wound for quicker, healthier healing. But I just couldn't. I don't think I was brave enough to stop, or maybe I was too brave so I kept pushing. Who knows? It doesn't even matter.

So here we are then, coming to terms with the knowledge that the gig is quite possibly up, and we need to think about our future together, our lives, childless.

Mr B was the first one to tentatively broach the subject. It's physically agonising, this part. I don't know if it's that way for everyone, but for me it feels like anticipatory torture, only exacerbated by the horrible fear of hope, and the accumulation of all of our previous failures. By now The Two Week Wait makes my insides twist and my toes curl involuntarily. I can only assume my husband feels something similar because he's grimacing as he turns to me and says, 'If this doesn't work, do we even have it in us to do it again?' My first thought is panic, because I have come to rely on my inability to stop. I absolutely, definitively cannot stop! But it's ridiculous to even wander down this path because I already know it's bullshit before I finish thinking it. We've run out of rope. We have a good life already, we love each other, we have a cat family and a nice gentle social life and if our future is just everything we already know, then that's OK, isn't it? Isn't it?

Only I don't know if it is, and that puts a hideous amount of pressure on us right now. On all four of us, really, while we start counting down the next two weeks until D-day. Because, oh yes, it's the full 14 days this time. When we were meeting with Dr Strauss in his office before the transfer, he told us to wait the maximum amount of time before doing the blood test that will indicate pregnancy or, well, no pregnancy. Which is new. Every other time we've been instructed to take the blood test on day 9 or day 11 sometimes, making it a one-and-a-half-week wait. Not quite as catchy. But, as Dr Strauss explained, it sets you up for extra anxiety. There is little point in testing so early and getting a tentative positive, which might drop off and become nothing a few days later. If you can hold on and test after the full two weeks, then you know if you get a positive, you can be quite confident in it.

I realise this may not be everyone's cup of tea. There are people who pee on little early-indicator strips every day to keep a close eye on the inside of their uterus, but I just couldn't handle the stress. Too much opportunity for fluctuating emotional extremes that can totally change by the day. I wish I'd had this obvious advice before. Then we wouldn't have had to suffer through Lydia's low positive and entire weekend wait just to find out it was in fact a negative.

The downside is that we now have a solid 14 days to fester. A fortnight of undulating anxiety, knowing that this will be the last time we ever have to go through this again. I feel better and worse for knowing that. This is going to be the toughest one.

The only thing for it really is to get stuck into normality. There is a beautiful quote by a comic actor called Sid Caesar, which I happened across at around this time, on Instagram of course, because where else do inspirational quotes pop into our consciousness these days? I'd like to think it was a spiritual occurrence, delivered to me just when I needed it. Obviously, it was actually an algorithmic one, which means my phone is listening to me, but I appreciate it nonetheless. But I digress:

> In between goals is a thing called life that has to be lived and enjoyed.

I bloody love that. It's so perfectly soothing for IVFers, we should be handed it printed on a T-shirt when we sign up with our doctors. It's the only way to get through a Two Week Wait with your sanity intact, and so while I hang about between goals, I set about living and enjoying my thing called life. OK, living my life. OK, trying to live my life in between the damn goals. I throw myself into work, I say yes to every invitation that comes my way in order to fill my days, no, my minutes, with as much mind-blocking distraction as possible. I drink to get drunk, which is not something that has ever been on my agenda, but I can't actually take this anymore. This has to be the last time, it's not healthy.

As such, the two weeks actually go by in a blur that is too fast for my liking. I actually want to stave pregnancy test day off as much as possible. I've felt this way about results ever since my cancer diagnosis, and all the scans and pregnancy tests we've taken since have done nothing to reverse that severely unpleasant feeling. This time, because there is so much potential heartbreak looming, feels entirely comparable to those bad old days. I'm saying waiting to receive the test results tomorrow feels as terrifying as waiting to find out if my cancer had spread? Yep. This time, it really does.

The only way we have been able to stay sane is to tell ourselves we know this won't work. Preempt the let-down. Expect the worst. It's not a stretch by any means, because by now we're perpetually prepared for bad news, so it quite naturally feels like anything else would be a miracle. I suppose it's quite sad really, but this state of mind is where all of our hard work has brought us. Our odds have always been excellent, every single time we've tried before, even when it was me and my broken body going through the treatment, but the accumulative losses have meant that the concept of a rogue positive result now feels totally abstract, so intangible; nothing short of a miracle.

But it's here, it's tomorrow and I'm stringing the day out with more wine and more trashy mind-numbing TV because I don't want to go to bed anxious. I don't want to wake up tomorrow knowing I might go to bed that night, heartbroken.

What I would like to do is cuddle my husband for comfort, but it seems the gods of business travel have given up on our hopeless crusade, because he is away again for goodness' sake. He's alone, this time in Vienna, and I'm alone, not in bed yet even though it's gone one in the morning.

If I were superstitious I would be horrendously worried that this will be the third results day in a row he is abroad with work. Those didn't turn out well, so on top of missing each other when we really need to hold each other up, probably literally right now, it feels like an ominous sign. We so wanted this time to feel different, and yes of course it is because our new British surrogate is also on the same countdown in the same time zone, it doesn't *feel* like it, yet. It feels ... it feels ... oh, I can't stay awake any—

Ahh, it's morning! FUCK, it's morning. I hate nothing more than when reality hits to make your awakening the rudest it could possibly be. This morning it is positively primitive. I am already anxious before the sleep has been blinked away. It feels very physical, like a sickly, undulating rush through my body that settles in the back of my eyeballs and makes everything go fuzzy for a moment. Because of my very late night, I've been woken up by the text from Rebecca, letting us know she just left the blood test clinic. It is seven o' clock in the morning. She isn't messing around! It strikes me how lovely it is that she is as keen as mustard to put us all out of our misery as fast as possible. And also how she and Jack must have had some trouble sleeping themselves last night. This is huge for them, too. They're on their own journey, lest we forget, creating their own amazing story and memories, whichever way this thing goes. It's just a very different perspective to our one. It's probably a little more towards the thrilling end of the spectrum for them, because they've never been here before. And they have two gorgeous children already. Everything blurs as I well up at the thought of all three of her boys at home, waiting for her to come back from taking a pregnancy test for us. I'm so grateful right now, it hurts.

From experience, the torturous wait for results is usually four or five hours, but they warned Rebecca they're unusually busy today, so it might take longer. There has been a near-constant flurry of excited chat on our WhatsApp group, while we all try to talk each other off various ledges. Mr B has been asking again and again how Rebecca is feeling. I don't know why he does it to himself, but he's worried that any symptom might be a good or a bad sign, so he's just going round and round in circles.

How are you feeling right now Rebecca?

She tells the group she's fine, she's been having mild cramping all week, which she hopes was the feeling of the embryo implanting.

Mr B says:

284

> Yes, Lydia had cramping and it was her body rejecting
> the embryo.

I think of him in emotional dire straits over in Vienna
and I well up again. Poor guy. I message back:

> Well, the two times mine implanted I had cramping too,
> so there.

Of course he doesn't miss a beat and messages me on the
side to remind us both that my two implanting did not
end well, so cramping is definitely a bad sign. I can't
argue with him there, so I say nothing instead. And then
our chat goes deathly silent as the minutes tick by. It's
because none of us want to spark hope with a premature
text ping, indicating that we might have some news. No
one knows who is going to receive it first, but I can pretty
much guarantee we are all glued to our phones in each of
our independent locations.

Rebecca is the first to give in, but it's OK, she's a rookie
at this. It's four hours after the test, right around the time
we should be getting the results, were there no holdup.

> Anyone else going mad?

Oh she has *no* idea. I'm at home on the sofa, kidding
myself that I'm getting some work done, but still in my
pyjamas and involuntarily rocking back and forth in the
foetal position, which is quite apt. Christ, this is so horri-

285

ble. The absolute horriblest in fact. It's an entirely different waiting game when it's your very last chance.

Mr B sends back:

Can barely breathe.

I can't think of him like this, it's too much.

Why is it taking so long?

Now he's peppering the chat like a machine gun.

I can't take this anymore!

How are you feeling? Sick?

Rebecca chases the clinic for the results and then relays to the group that they'll be in at 2:30. It is now 1:15. Having a set time weirdly feels worse, like there's no point obsessively refreshing my emails anymore, so what the hell else am I supposed to do with myself? I spend a productive twenty minutes staring at nothing, and then go back to refreshing emails, because that is my pregnancy test results day compulsion.

I'm refreshing and refreshing and refreshing until, suddenly, earlier than expected, an email comes in with the subject line:

BERESINER RESULTS

I'm struggling to use my laptop touchpad because my heart is beating out of my chest and my hands are shaking hard. It's an encrypted secure email for goodness' sake! I have to click a link and input my password. I don't think I have a password? Do I? I can't think! Surely it's dangerous for someone's heart to beat this hard and fast … argh, am I going to pass out?

While I'm still grappling with the email – I literally can't focus on the screen – my phone also pings. Rebecca obviously has a password, because she sends a screenshot of the opened email to the group WhatsApp with a note saying:

I've got the results but I can't understand them.

I, with a lot of previous experience, scan the sheet from the lab quickly, and finally take the breath I'd been holding.

Well.

I guess miracles do happen.

* * *

OK. OK, OK, I need to think. I don't know what I expected to feel but it certainly was not this, because I sort of feel stuck. Like my needle's hit a rough spot. I'm not sure this can be right, because what I'm staring at on the sheet, the numbers that I've been blinking and blinking again to clear my vision to see properly, still look like they might be a typo. I can't get this wrong because I need to translate to the group what it says, especially Mr B, who by all rights should be here with me.

> Levels greater than 5.8 indicate positive. I think it says the
> level is 1112. Can that be right? I'm shaking, can
> someone please clarify?

Because 1112 is waaay greater than 5.8.

Jack jumps in from the staffroom at his school, where he's surreptitiously texting under the table.

> That's how I'm reading it.

Mr B is in the middle of a big meeting in Vienna, and so he types,

> I can't read it!!

I can feel nervous tension seeping through every letter.
Rebecca then types:

> I calleeee Lucg.

I think Rebecca is having an adrenaline spike, I think Rebecca is saying she'll call Lucy at the clinic to clarify. There's not even time for me to finish typing out 'Call her please!' before she pings back with:

PREGNANT.

Pregnant.

I let that word percolate for a moment. My instinct is to be afraid, of course it is, because I've had positives before. I've toasted them with champagne and added maternity dresses to my shopping bag and then look what happened. OK my numbers were low, around the 75 mark. Our last surrogate Lydia's was on the absolute cusp at 5.9. I don't know how we even dared hope with that one. So I'm more than aware that this does not mean celebration time just yet. And then, while still blinking at the screen, I remember Dr Strauss telling us that if we get a positive after 14 days we can be confident in it. I feel a flutter in my stomach that surges up to settle in my clenched jaw. I remember the hCG hormone reading being so high that I still think it might be a typo. Is that representative of the confidence he promised us? I can't quite, um, I don't know what to ... I don't know what to say! Oh my. What the hell do you say in that moment, what is big enough to capture this feeling via the disjoined medium of WhatsApp, to this eclectic collection of people who have managed to do what feels like the impossible on our very last chance? After all we did to try and please,

please make this one happen. After four years of heart-break and hard work?

OMFG

Says I.

OMFG

Says Mr B at the exact same time. We are nothing if not cosmically attuned.

Lucy at Mr Hiyer's practice emailed Rebecca back to say her levels are absolutely great at 1112 (so it definitely isn't a typo!) and they'll want her to repeat the blood test in a few days to make sure the numbers are doubling. OK, this is the first hurdle we need to clear because doubling numbers indicates the pregnancy is progressing in the right direction. Static or declining numbers, which we've experienced three times before, mean the opposite. Therefore I will be holding my breath for the next 48 hours but, as far as we know, everything looks better than good. Right now, REBECCA IS PREGNANT!!!

I think I must be experiencing some shock because I can't manage to squeeze out a single tear. Apart from being incredibly frustrating – it's like I'm about to burst – it's making me feel a bit guilty. Rebecca and Jack are abso-lutely over the moon, and so they should be, and I want her to see how emotionally fulfilled she has made me. I want to burst the dam so she can see tangible evidence, but we are so burnt by the past and it's really hard to relax. I shake myself and suggest we all take a picture of ourselves right in this moment and keep it for posterity, and for the baby. (The baby!) Rebecca sends a very sweet photo of her mock-shocked, absolutely beaming with her youngest son in the background pulling a similar expression. I send mine, make-up-free, sat on the sofa still in my PJs and, if you look closely, you can definitely see the fear behind my eyes. Jack is in the staffroom so he sends a surreptitious selfie, and Mr B, in his now empty conference room, is just about ready to collapse. They are *so* special and funny, I love these stills. I love how dazed I look and how floppy Mr B looks and how excited and happy Rebecca and Jack look.

And still no tears. My eyes are practically itching in protest. I need to speak to my mum and dad because obviously they need to be the first to know, and there is nothing like some parental comfort to get the tear ducts going. Also, they knew when I went to Washington. I have stopped keeping my nearest and dearest totally abreast of everything that's going on, because I can't deal with everyone else's pity and disappointment. It's too much pressure to add to the results day pot. But they can do the maths. Even though we didn't explicitly tell them the test date, they counted to fourteen too, and will also have woken up holding their collective breath this morning.

My mum picks up Dad's mobile on the first ring, telling me they're about to go into a funeral service for one of her university friends, so what do I need? Obviously they have been clutching that phone to their chests at all times, because who answers on their way into a funeral? I quickly get to the point.

'Mum, it worked! Rebecca is pregnant!' I can barely believe I'm saying it out loud.

'Oh!' she gasps. And then, 'I'm scared!' She's using a funny kind of exhilarated voice.

And this is the absolute truth of the matter. We have come so far, we've been through every step of it together, because that is how this family dynamic works now, ever since my cancer. It's amazing how a life-changing experience like that can totally alter an already close relationship. This, today, is so *fucking amazing*. It's absolutely incredible news, it's a miracle result, on our very last chance, and it just feels like someone is waiting to take it away again. We all feel it. Damn you traumatic IVF history. Don't you bring my mum into this.

The crux of it is that this will have been the fourth positive pregnancy result we've had in the last four years of trying, but it is definitely the one that means the most. Since the others didn't progress as we hoped, we all need to keep our happy news-ometers in check until we know if it is indeed medically 'viable'. And the first indicator of that will be the next blood test.

I go to work on the next blood test day and set about pretending to be a supremely capable member of staff. I go to meetings with bright eyes and I nod and blink at the right times, but that is the limit of my capacity. I can't hear anything anyone is saying, I cannot distract myself from this one, but I pretend. I pretend I am calmly detached from my phone – that is sat within view at all times – and its impending 'ping'.

'Ping!!'

It's Rebecca.

Holy shit, look at your phones people.

Apparently we have the results emailed to us all, but I don't need to look at my phone because she follows up with:

It's 5644. We are still very much pregnant.

And boom, just like that we are in entirely new territory. We've never been here before, never this many bouts of good news in a row. Now it feels real. Now I suddenly get why people drink a whisky in moments of acute intensity. Once the meeting is finished, I go across the road to my favourite after-work hang-out and ask the bartender to pour a finger. I sip it slowly and feel my bones warming. Reality is settling into them, and I have a little giggle to myself. I'm a whisky-drinking expectant mother. I'm already breaking the rules.

19.
The end?

It seems crazy that a tiny thing without any discernible extremities can have a heart, but it should do – a two-chamber heart that looks like a tube twisted back on itself. If all is still well in two weeks', that is. As long as the embryo hasn't reabsorbed into the uterus lining and left behind an empty gestational sac, which can happen, but let's not dwell on that too hard, OK?

I can't help it, I now spend every day worrying for *everyone* in this scenario who has so much invested in it working out in the end. Which will technically be the beginning.

And now it feels like we're gambling chips on the blackjack table. Every time we win, now the stakes get higher, and the farther we've gone, the more people we've collected to share the spoils.

Strangely enough for a family that has become ridiculously close going through this whole thing, we spend much of the next fortnight kind of avoiding each other. I'm reluctant to call home because I hear the panic in my parents' voices every time they pick up the phone to me.

The end?

They're expecting bad news, of course. We all are, because that's been our pattern for years now. So, it's easier not to call them.

Rebecca and Jack are doing great. They gathered their two boys on the sofa to tell them the amazing news that they've both been waiting for right along with us, and they filmed it to send to us. It's utterly wonderful. She starts with, 'So. Do you remember when you met Sophie and her husband?'

'Mm hmm.'

'And how much they wanted a baby? And how much we thought we would help them by using my tummy?'

'Mm hmmmmm.'

'Well, guess what? The baby's in my tummy!'

They gasp and the older one says, 'Ah! Let's, let's see?' while the younger one turns his attention back to his yoghurt biscuit.

She explains they can't see because it's still growing so she doesn't have a big fat tummy yet, but do they think it's good news? Yeah they do!

Jack asks if they have anything to say about it and their eldest breaks my heart in two with: 'We're very lucky that we were the ones to be chosen to help them.'

I'm pretty sure right now that we are the lucky ones.

I still worry for Mr B, every day, because he refuses to let himself feel hopeful, even when I explain how positive the hormone level readings are again, and how this time feels totally different. But it just doesn't for him, he's too traumatised by the past to let his guard down just yet. He spends his free moments buried in research and statistics, calculating when it is going to be OK to really believe in this thing. And he concludes that it definitely isn't yet. Actually, Mr B's lateral thinking is pretty useful at this point, because it helps to take the emotion out of the situation. He could channel his anxiety into IVF merchandise to help others succumbing to their over-emotional over-thinking. Statistics-based wallcharts, emotionally neutral affirmations or something. 'My thoughts are peaceful and calm. I completely love and trust my body. There are success percentages attached to each milestone of this journey and a conversion percentage at every stage.'

I worry for Dr Strauss and his coordinator Annabel who have gone out of their way to offer us this best last chance, and are so thrilled that we're still in the game. And Emma the acupuncturist and my sister and Rebecca and Jack's kids, and every friend who has cried with us when it hasn't worked before. And try as I might not to, I worry for me, for how much more I have to lose with every hope-building day that passes.

And right now, I'm especially worried for Mr Hiyer and his team, because it's time for the last big hurdle. Rebecca, Mr B and I are in his office for the seven-week heartbeat scan to finally establish whether this is a medically viable pregnancy or, well, it isn't, and this is the end of the road. To have to deliver that kind of awful news to us must be a horrendous pressure in itself. He would be so upset, I know he would, after all this time we've spent together, the years he has put into trying to help and support us. STOP! I have to stop. There is no point in going there, but I recognise now it is just where my mind finds itself going. I hope beyond hope that today, these next few minutes, will determine the exact time that bad, sad habit goes away.

So here we are, Mr B and I interestingly and unusually in the exact same place for this next part of the story: two non-pregnant people willing our baby to come into the world healthy. Until I become the mum, I guess I get to live the traditional 'other half' experience. It's a nice, comforting feeling, that we're really in it together in more senses than most, a problem halved and all that.

If today Mr Hiyer hears a healthy heartbeat, it apparently reduces the chance of miscarriage to just 5 per cent. I find myself staring at Rebecca and obsessing about the idea of a tiny, delicate, living person becoming itself, in her belly. With a heartbeat! I've always thought that making babies was miraculous, but thinking about it in the biological detail that controlled IVF affords us, with such a precise and scientific timeline, is just nuts. It's awesome. So please let there be a heartbeat. There has to be one, little one. We are already referring to you endearingly and familiarly, in every conversation. You have to be alive right now.

And to be honest, I have been feeling quietly confident about that. Right up until now, that we're in the room. Over the last couple of weeks the signs have been good. Rebecca has been having increasingly worse morning sickness, which is not wildly great for her, but even so, she finds it as thrilling as we do. She has been going for regular acupuncture appointments with Emma, who then messages me to say: 'Pulses feeling excellent.' She, by the way, was able to tell both times I was pregnant just a few days after implantation, just by feeling my pulse. I sometimes think Chinese medicine is about as miraculous as baby making. 'That's good, right?' I message back. 'Yep! The energy has shifted baby, you are on a new trajectory.' I'm elated because I trust Emma and her holistic soothing ways wholeheartedly.

When we met Rebecca in the waiting room just before we came in, she reassured us wasn't nervous, but I think I know her by now. She's definitely looking a bit peaky, although that could be the morning sickness. She is feeling it, too. And now that we're all collected here together, at the most pivotal moment possible, even Mr Hiyer seems to be slightly wobbly.

'Hello, hello, hi,' he says, as he perfunctorily shakes us each by the hand a little too enthusiastically. Then he smooths his tie and sits down at his desk before immediately standing back up again. 'Right!' he says. 'Shall we do this, then?'

I'm touched that he's obviously nervous too and it strikes me that he must have to deliver bad news at this point fairly regularly. Oh God, what if it's bad news? Mr B has to take a seat all of a sudden – we think alike, that's for sure – and so once again, Rebecca and I do the Dignity Dance.

The end?

Mr Hiyer's office is a lovely big room with a beautiful screen partitioning off the stirrups chair, equipment and screen from the rest of the space, including the sofa where Mr B is perched.

I've had scans in Hiyer's office myself, so I know that you have to take everything off from the waist down and that the stirrups face the partition, so I'm loath to peek around in case I see the things I'm sure she would prefer only her husband and gynaecologist see. I stay standing on the other side, trying to hold it together, eyes and shaky camera phone fixed firmly on the wall-mounted TV in front of us. Some indeterminate space scene comes on the screen and moves around until a tiny black blob appears. I have no idea what I'm looking at, Mr B can't look at all, and there is bone-jangling silence for a painfully long few seconds, until, finally Mr Hiyer says in a rush of exhaled breath: '*There* it is – ah yes – good strong heartbeat, there we GO!'

It's there! Look. There it is. A tiny, fluttering little shadow that, wait, where? He points it out again. Still not sure what I'm looking at and really keen to remember this image forever, I ask him to show me just one more time? Oh yes, I see it! (I absolutely don't see it, but I trust it is there and I don't like to ruin the moment.)

Plus Rebecca is yelling to Mr B over the partition, 'Are you OK?'

He is actually more than OK, I know this just by looking at him. On the inside anyway. The outside is a sobbing mass of joy and relief, and now that I think about it, I notice that my own face is somewhat contorted, and my throat is tight and my cheeks are damp, too. I do an audible sob and Rebecca laughs from behind the screen, clearly happy that we are finally doing the crying we've been holding in since we met her.

Mr Hiyer comes round the partition and invites us to join him at his desk while Rebecca gets dressed; he is positively beaming. Then we all sit down and try to keep it together while he tells us the growing foetus (it's a foetus!) is the exact right size, it all looks absolutely excellent, and although we're only at seven weeks, we can 'definitely take the breath we've been holding.'

I feel it rush through me like crystal cold water. My god this feels good. This feels better than I even expected. Better than I could ever have imagined creating a baby could be.

While I'm lost in my own unbridled joy, Mr B, being Mr B, makes a very astute point, because we're some way off the traditional 12-week mark: is he sure it's going to be OK? 'So, when do you think it's safe to start telling people?'

Mr Hiyer looks at us each one at a time, and says with a massive smile: 'If it were me, I'd be shouting it from the rooftops.'

So here we are, wind in our hair. Pass me the megaphone, please. 'Hello? Is this thing on? *clears throat, takes deep breath* 'WE'RE HAVING A BLOODY BABY!'

Epilogue

The thing with infertility is that there are way too many variables – too many emotions and people and feelings and hurdles – to make it comparable to anyone else's experience. Mr B and I have reached the end of this as quite different people, changed by the four years it took to get here, to our beginning again. I have so much to look forward to and, at the same time, I suspect I might crumble unexpectedly at a wholly inconvenient time. Like in the middle of the school nativity play I've been longing to have in my future. Or mid-cappuccino as I write the final sentences of this book in the cafe at the end of my street. But I'm here. I'm waiting for you, my *daughter*. And I'm so overwhelmed by that, there's not a single other thing to say about it. Other than I can't wait for you to be able to read this one day and know how much you were loved by so many people right from the start of our story. You had an entourage before you had a heartbeat. And we're sorry we spent your inheritance on your existence, but, them's the breaks kid. Now go and tidy your room.

Acknowledgements

I should probably start at the beginning, even though it starts and ends the same way.

To my beautiful Mr B. You, one of the more private people on the planet, gave me permission to write about our most personal struggles and publish them in a national newspaper. I gave you copy approval and I even listened to your feedback. Even episodes on the fly. But nothing within these covers would've been possible without you. From the precision project management to the proofreading; from your passionately protective nature, right down to the person you helped create. I love our daughter all the more because she is part of you. Lucky us, eh? Thank you for saying yes to almost everything. (Can we watch a movie now, please?)

A huge thank you to pre-existence Marlies, my muse. And to real-life Marlies, for napping to something resembling a schedule so that your mamma could write about you in between loving life with you. You are officially the centre of my universe.

Thank you dear Rebecca, you angel of the north. You are so much more exceptional than you know, you know, and nothing will ever change that fact for any of us. You'll hate this, I'll shut up now. And to Jack, our fourth wheel (aka the important one that stops the whole cart toppling over).

My wonderful mum and dad. Despite the set of circumstances that laid the foundation for this book, having you my whole life means no one can ever really describe me as unlucky. It's impossible to express my appreciation in words, but I'll keep trying. I love you a ridiculous amount, and so does your granddaughter! Thank you for being there through it all with me. (And I'll always be sorry about that, too.)

Thank you to my brilliant agent Kate, who always gets me. For all the inappropriately late and weekend WhatsApps and for beautifully articulating exactly what I'm thinking. It's fair to say I totally got my money's worth with you, eh?

To my editor(s) at HarperCollins for believing in doing things differently in this traditionally sad space, and the brilliant team who have championed the book with bells on: Katya Shipster, Helen Rochester and Sarah Hammond. Julie MacBrayne and Josie Turner. To the poor design team who I annoyed the hell out of, sorry and thank you at the same time.

To Marlies' entourage, our A-team: Rebecca, Jack, Mr B. Amazing Adrian and his wonderfully caring team. Emma my soul sister. Michael, Amanda and every brilliant person at SFG. Billie Dee our saviour, and Ayehsa Vardag, Kathryn and Emma, thank you. Katie, your cooking was outstanding! Dan, Levi and Theo, mazel tov to you too. The midwives (all of them) at Barnet Hospital. And egg donor no. 234 who will never know it's our lives she's been such a big part of.

To Lesley and Harriet for taking a punt and making TMP a thing in the first place. Thank you to Laura and my editors at *Sunday Times Style*, and to my mate Hannah Swerls for helping me shape that original column pitch (remember?), then coming full circle to be my intermittent and brilliant boss for a bit.

Thank you Pete, my great friend and pretty much personal photographer by now too. Smashed it out the park while our tea got cold, didn't we?

And the biggest thank you to every reader, commentator, proponent, anonymous or otherwise, for being my support network until I had the family you all willed me towards. It worked.

Ahh, my beautiful family. Thank you. I love you.